Witch

and the

Wildwood

Folk Wisdom, Fairy Tale & Fantastic Lore

Sarah Robinson

WOMANCRAFT PUBLISHING

Published by Womancraft Publishing, 2024
www.womancraftpublishing.com

ISBN 978-1-910559-94-9
The Witch and the Wildwood is also available in ebook format:
ISBN 978-1-910559-93-2

Cover image © Olya Luki. Instagram @luki.olya
Illustrations: Lucy H. Pearce

Womancraft Publishing is committed to sharing powerful new women's voices, through a collaborative publishing process. We are proud to midwife this work, however the story, the experiences and the words are the author's alone. A percentage of Womancraft Publishing profits are invested back into the environment reforesting the tropics (via TreeSisters) and forward into the community.

A percentage of royalties from this book supports the reforestation projects of Tree-Sisters – www.treesisters.org

PRAISE FOR
THE WITCH AND THE WILDWOOD

*This charming book takes the reader's hand and leads
them to the wild, where possibilities lurk. Perfect
for the adventurer, or the fireside-voyager.*

Alice Tarbuck, author of *A Spell in the Wild*

*Sarah Robinson skilfully guides readers into the dark and
enchanted forest, following the scary trails of fairy tales and ancient
myths, discovering fairies and monsters, teaching trees and Earth
Goddesses, antlered Gods and Green Men, and finding Witches,
the wise and untamed women whose holy, healing magic will
transform you into the magical being you are meant to be.*

**Phyllis Curott, Witch, author of *Spells for Living Well*,
the *Witches' Wisdom Tarot*, and *Book of Shadows***

*In this magical treasure of a book, we encounter the sorceresses,
priestesses, witches, and Sibyls from days gone by, their voices alive in
landscape and stone. We can hear them, soothsayers and wise women
who shaped continents and raised temples and sang wild prayers
across the land under a deepening moon. We can feel them and we
can hear them, because they're still here, we're still here, witches in the
wildwood, still making the magic, still tending the flame, still telling
the story, still singing the song, still listening to magic at work in the
world. This book helps us to connect, to claim, and to remember. This
book is a work of both liberation and of reclamation. A powerful
journey into story and power, myth and magic, earth and sky,
memory and change, land and courage, enchantment and discovery.*

**Molly Remer, author of *Womanrunes*, *Walking with
Persephone*, and *365 Days of Goddess*, creatrix of
the #30DaysofGoddess devotional practice**

Sarah takes your hand and leads you deep into the dark wildness of the forest. There she introduces the otherworldly creatures who dwell in those wild and secret spaces, including goddesses, gods, wildalones, green men, and – of course – witches!

The inclusion of lesser known folktales and lore from the British Isles and Northern Europe is magic, and makes The Witch and the Wildwood a fun and engaging frolic through those shadowy spaces others try to avoid.

Jessica M Starr, author of *Waking Mama Luna*

Other books by Sarah Robinson

Yoga for Witches
Yin Magic: How to be Still
Kitchen Witch: Food, Folklore & Fairy Tale
Enchanted Journeys: Guided Meditations for Magical Transformation

In collaboration with Lucy H. Pearce:

The Kitchen Witch Companion: Recipes, Rituals & Reflections

CONTENTS

OPENING – **Page 1**
Wildwood – Once Upon a Time – Entering the Wild – Meeting the Witch –
Remembering Folklore – Reclaiming Magic – Let's Wander and Wonder

1 – INTO THE WOODS – **Page 13**
A Magical Life – Disenchantment – A Rekindling –
Fairy Tale – Real and Fictional Woods

2 – THE WITCH OF THE WILDWOOD IN
FOLKLORE & FAIRY TALE – **Page 33**
Ancient Wise Ones – Witchcraft and Treelore – The Edge of the Unknown –
Revealing the Wyrd

3 – OTHER MAGICAL INHABITANTS OF THE WILDWOOD
– **Page 55**
The Wildalones – The Huldra – Wood-Wives and Witch Maidens – Vengeful
Spirits – The Green Man and Wild Men – Bogles – Marsh Witches – Monsters

4 – GODS & GODDESSES OF THE WILDWOOD – **Page 85**
The Antlered Gods of the Greenwood – Classical Goddesses of the Forest –
Goddesses from Northern European Folklore – Ancient and Modern

5 – REAL WITCHES OF THE WILDWOOD – **Page 109**
Witches on Trial – The Pendle Witches – Dancing in Dark Forests – Witch
Pyres – Unorthodox Religious Practice – Modern Witches of the Wildwood
– Unoffical and Unconventional

6 – WOMEN WHO RUN WITH THE WOLVES – **Page 131**
The Wild Woman Archetype – A Wild Woman Awakens – Wolves and
Goddesses – Wolf Mothers and Werewolves – Power and Prejudice
– To be a Wild Woman – The Modern Wild Woman

CLOSING – **Page 151**
Inspiring Change – Wild Entanglement – Rewilding Our Stories

OPENING

WILDWOOD

The wildwood seems to somehow cradle magic in its branches: swirling mist and hanging vines, crunching forest floors and honeyed sunlight soaking through banks of ferns. Even those of us who live in urban jungles and concrete cities can easily bring to mind the scent of pine needles, earth and moss. That sense of feeling very small amongst centuries old trees that are taller and older than some cathedral spires. And just as easily brought to mind are a tale or two about the dark woods, first heard in childhood, that have filled these unknown spaces with mythic and mysterious beings that crawl, lurk and fly through the wildwood.

"Wildwood" is an evocative word. It has been used as a technical descriptor by ecologists, as well as by writers and playwrights to capture the feeling of unruly and unfamiliar spaces. The term "wildwood" is used to refer to woodland growing in the wild, natural state; it can be found referred to in old English manuscripts in Middle English as *wilde wode/weldewode,* and Old English *wilde wudu.* There are many other beautiful and ancient woodland words too: greenwood (woods or forest when green, as in summer) and tanglewood (literally tangled woods, branches, briers, vines) and the evocative mirkwood (dense woodland, the term is drawn from old Norse *Myrkvior* meaning dark wood – anglicised to mirkwood and famously used by author J.R.R. Tolkien).

The term "wildwood" appears in medieval and Renaissance literature, epic poems, ballads, and romantic tales, like Arthurian legends and the writings of Shakespeare. It was popularised as a modern term by ecologist Oliver Rackham to denote Britain's natural tree cover and is now commonly used for remaining fragments of ancient woodland, uncultivated woods or forest that has been allowed to grow naturally. One could argue that no woodlands are entirely free from human influence thanks to climate change, and Rackham himself said true wildwood no longer exists in the British Isles. But it is a word still used commonly today so I'm going to take some liberties and use it abundantly for wild and wooded spaces both in the real world and in story. Some may see woods as friendly – such as the Hundred-Acre Wood of Winnie the Pooh and friends, with woodland glades and friendly creatures, whereas forests might be thought of as more wild and unruly – the Black Forest, Sherwood Forest, the New Forest – with battles fought and children lost. But each wooded space holds tales of myth and magic, witches and wild creatures. What truly makes a wildwood perhaps, is not the size or even its age, but the stories within...

The wildwood can be generous: for foraging, hiking, and healing, but it has never been a place that one should venture into mindlessly. With technological advancements, we may well be able to venture further and deeper into the forests and repel wild animals. But in earlier centuries, the wildwood held more haunting unknowns: it was both a place of marvels and perils, of exclusion and refuge for outcasts, criminals and supernatural beings. One did not venture into the forest without good reasons; those who did risked never returning. Children across cultures and ages have been warned of the dangerous beings that lie within: stories that can be told just right to instil enough fear to ensure caution, and yet seed enough mystery to spark wonder.

TREE TALES

While this book is an exploration of the wildwood as a larger concept rather than individual trees of the woods, please excuse me *branching out* into a few snippets of specific tree lore that I couldn't resist including. Every tree species has its own wonderful lore: some connected to the healing properties or characteristics of the tree, how one might use the wood or berries for charms or rituals, stories of trees that may be connected to gods or spirits, offerings that may be made to the trees or simply interesting tales that may have grown up around areas where one species of tree may be prevalent.

> In practices of folk magic and herbal medicine, each tree has its own unique properties, and various parts of trees – leaves, bark, twigs, sap, flowers and berries – have been used in spells, charms and remedies for healing, protection, and also in ritual and divination. Some accused of being witches were said to have used parts of trees in their magical practices. Though the woods were a rich source of medicinal herbs and plants used by everyone, in superstition it was only witches in their practices, and so accusations could be made based on the gathering of herbs or the possession of knowledge related to herbalism.

Once Upon a Time...

Once upon a time, woods and forests were at the heart of daily life. The seasons governed daily routines, and people generally lived much more closely with the natural world. Forests, hedgerows and meadows provided fuel, food, building materials, grazing pasture and medicines. The woods provided wild harvests of nuts, fruits and game meat and people made livelihoods out of its resources, living with and honouring seasonal rhythms as a necessity.

Although few actually lived in the very centre of wild spaces, the wild was more present in the minds of communities – as somewhere that needed to be travelled through, skirted around, hidden in, utilised for food or fuel, or avoided at night. Woods were laced with cart tracks and trails, and people journeyed through, from holloways to hunting paths and they were mapped by distinctive landmarks: the tallest of the trees, rocky outcrops wrapped in ivy, fallen trunks and roots decayed into shapes suggestive enough to earn nicknames, winding brooks, bogs and the ruins of older hearths and walls.

Many have attempted to capture this wildwood wonder with stories of enchantment, that seek to convey the special energy and importance of woodlands through characters of myth and magic. The magical beings of the woods are part of a rich history of story used by our ancestors to explore what the woods are and what it is about them that may create such variety of emotion, from feelings of joy and safety to reverence and fear.

How have different cultures and eras explained this idea of the wildwood? What do these stories tell us about how people and societies saw and interacted with the woods? This is what I seek to explore in this book: to journey through the wilds, through magic, lore, trees and woods. To explore what wildness and the magic within it meant to ancient Greeks and Romans, pagans, heathens and Celts, from the medieval peasant and farmer to modern era poets, authors and artists. I'll be mainly exploring my homelands of Britain and Europe in this book as realms I know best, though every country and culture has folklore of wild nature worth exploring, and some cultures still work closely with the land and their ancestral practices. I know some will be disappointed that beautiful stories of the woodlands of Africa and Asia, for example, don't feature in this book; others would be equally disappointed and angry if I, a native European, spoke to the relevance of folklore in cultures that are not mine. If either the inclusion or absence of stories inspires you to seek more of your own tales and histories, I will consider this book a success.

Here you will find a wildwood of stories, winding explorations, wild ideas and wonder-filled tales. Elders loom and willows dance, and wonderful beings weave between them. This is a journey through how, when we look upon a swathe of trees, certain folk see wonder, whilst others feel repulsion. There are obvious challenges like cold, rain, bugs, fear of getting lost that may make some (okay, many!) of us a little trepidatious when approaching a dense wood. But there's more I think – a sense that dark woods can hold things, things that drift into the edges our awareness from memory, myth, folklore and fairy tales – and real history as well – it is not just in the realms of fairy tale that people get lost in the woods. The dangers one may meet can range from human, animal to something more unexplainable and even magical.

Entering the Wild

The wild means different things to different people in different contexts: natural, untamed, chaotic, uncontrolled, untended, free... The opposite of wild is civilised, man-made, domesticated, controlled, obedient. This book is an exploration of what it is to be called wild, to work with the wild, to seek the wild in various ways and how the wild can change you. There is a paradox here: the wild is both a place of fear and trepidation, and a luring, lovely place, a place of bounty and hunger, peril and delight. Where there is the unknown there is possibility and freedom. Perhaps these stories may prompt you to look again, or see something a little differently, new or enchanting amongst the trees. No matter how wild or familiar the wood.

If my books on the Kitchen Witch (published in 2022 and 2023) were about the sacredness and enchantment held within the domestic realm of kitchen, hearth, garden and home, this book is surely the wild twin, exploring enchantment of the wildwood and forest and how often through time we have used such figures as the wild feminine and the witch to embody the untamed nature of wild places. There are powerful ideas to be found within the wildwood to inspire, enchant and treasure. There is magic in journeying through story, myth, legend, and so much to find, you never really know where it will take you.

Dante finds himself lost at the beginning of his poem "The Inferno" (1314):

"In the middle of our life's path
I found myself in a dark forest,
Where the straight way was lost."

I'll be honest with you, dear reader, I've lost my way several times writing this book and got tangled in the roots of what I actually want to say, what I want the book to be. I had ideas at first of a rather serene book listing the folklore and tales of different trees and plants with a friendly cover that might sit on the shelves of cosy National Trust shops and country stores. But as so often happens when I write a book, the stories have taken me somewhere quite different – and what has transpired instead is a journey through the 'wild' and what that means.

The wild, I found, like the word witch, can't be held down too tightly; that's when the edges begin to bleed, and everything I thought I knew was thrown into the half-light and liminal places. I will do my best to keep to a straight path, but, fair warning, wanderings do occur! And each creates just one more thread of this wild journey, like getting lost in the woods…

MEETING THE WITCH

We can find the female form dwelling in multitude in the forests of folklore and fairy tale – witches, nymphs, fairies and other hidden folk – personifying the natural world's power to entice, enchant, frighten and deceive.

Why do so many of our collective stories of woods and trees also feature – in addition to wild creatures – magical ones: witches, mythic creatures and fairy folk. This is the lore that rises when the light of the day fades, and the ancient myths begin to scratch and scuttle at the edges of imagination and memory. In dim light in the heart of the woods the mysteries deepen somehow, as do its dangers when we look through these enchanting tales of hope and fears that cling to the boundaries of our collective consciousness. There are vast numbers of archetypes, characters and deities tied in with the storied history of our natural world, and as usual, my bias is for exploring the feminine in those stories, which has often been unfairly demonised.

Our guide is ever-present, my lodestar lens through which I look at these stories: the witch. The witch, as both a historical figure and an enduring archetype, is the figure perhaps most commonly connected with the wildwood. As we travel together, we will see many of her different faces – historical, malevolent, murderous, protective, enchanting and empowering – as we explore a wealth of stories involving the witch and the wildwood. The number of different things people think and feel about witches is near infinite. Some inspirational, some horrifying, some tediously predictable, misogynistic, belittling, dismissive or ill-informed. When I speak of "witch" I do so in awareness of: the innocent accused of the witch trials, people who claim the title witch today, and the witch of stories and superstitions long told. To say the word "witch" somehow encompasses them all, and much more.

What does the presence of the witch in the wild show to us? Of us? That's the crux of it. And through these chapters I will explore as best I can, the stories held within the wild with the witch as guide – via all manner of folk myth, superstition and true events. How were real women perceived as wild and accused as witches? How and why were witches portrayed in fiction and folk and fairy tales as connected to the wildwoods? What did it mean to be a witch in the past...and what does it mean to embody the archetype of wild woman today?

The witch's wild nature has always been a symbol of a certain unruliness. I am fascinated by how the witch has been woven through stories of the wildwoods. Perhaps because, to so many, the woods are like these witches, women, and wild souls: we both fear them and seek them out, and they cannot be entirely controlled.

The witch has so many faces. One of the many reasons why she is so enigmatic and fascinating (and terrifying as well) is that some of those faces were those of real people – like Elizabeth Southerns and Anne Whittle, some were amalgamations of folk and fairy tales like Baba Yaga, and others were myths from civilisations long dead, but the stories of them all help us gain an understanding into how the wild feminine has been seen and treated by our cultures.

Together we will delve more deeply into how and why the witch and the wildwoods are so closely woven together – in temperaments (unpredictable, fearsome), potential for magic (healing, transformation, enchantment, reverence) and even appearance (gnarled, weathered, wrinkled), mirroring each other in many stories. Why do we see wild nature in the witch, and the witch in wild nature? We have long found dual forces of both intrigue and reticence in the forest and its dwellers – both living and folkloric. This journey, travelling through wilderness and enchantment, will, I hope, bring us, at times, face-to-face with the witch (no mean feat) and many elusive creatures who dwell beyond the edges of 'ordinary' life and civilisation. In meeting these esoteric figures, we can learn a little more of our irrational fears, our own inner wildness, our relationship to the natural world, what captures our imagination, our sense of wonder and better understand our own nature and place in the world.

Remembering Folklore

We will explore the magical and folkloric histories of some of Europe's most fascinating forests and wild spaces. I'll arrange the stories into broad categories exploring the story of wildwoods and loss of rural way of life, tales of witches and wild women, mythical dwellers and deities of the woods, historical witches and the archetype of wild woman in contemporary culture – each offering its own perspective. This is an invitation to be enchanted and engage with stories and histories, the joyful and delightful as well as the sorrowing and terrifying.

I have delighted in uncovering some particularly beautiful wildwood stories from folk and fairy tale from many sources. These are stories that have travelled far, through many centuries and countless cultures. I retell them in my own words with humility and respect: for this moment, in this place, I am their carrier. These are not my stories: these are *our* stories, stories that travel, stories that endure, stories that tell us more about ourselves, our primal selves – our hopes, dreams, fears, longings – and the unseen realms of the world we inhabit, with warning for how to best proceed.

As best I can, and as often as I can, I'll share words of women* and how wise women, 'old wives', crones, foragers, herbalists, hags and healers saw the wildwood and how others connected them to the woods. And how these varied people found the spirit of place in the wildwood (and the Spirits of place, in many cases).

Folk culture speaks to a sense of enchantment and identification with the land, which is often lacking in our modern lives. Folk tales connect us to a rich and ancient heritage that is available to us all – no matter how urban our landscape. However small the wild spaces we can access, wherever we come across trees, wildflowers, 'weeds' or grass, the whispers of dryads, fairies and the Green Man can be found because they do not belong to one place, one single vision of 'the wild', but in our own stories and imaginings, our own ideas of what magic is. The witch stood, and still stands, as one embodiment of such magic, along with many beasts, deities, spirits and the vast, feral wilds. She may haunt secluded corners, sowing dread in the hearts of unsuspecting travellers or offer a guiding light, hope or possibility. This witch and her kin cast lingering shadows across the corners of the world. Society is ever-changing, but the witch remains in the fabric of modern imagination, casting a witch's light[†] through folklore and imagination. Perhaps these stories will enchant your next journey to the trees, offering a light to shine on the residual magic that still dwells within our memories and ancestry that can re-enchant our daily lives.

---

* Whatever your gender identity, it is my intention and hope that you'll find some interesting ideas and magical tales here. Looking back into older stories and folklore of the medieval era into early modern era, we find that a huge percentage of witches in stories and accused witches in history were women, and in fairy tales there is certainly a fondness for wicked stepmothers and evil sorceresses. So, you will find a leaning toward feminine pronouns – as is historically accurate. But fear not, we will also meet liminal beings, wise men, wild men and masculine hunters carousing through these pages, as well as archetypal ideas such as the wild woman that can speak to us all.

† "Witch light" or "witches' lantern" are terms that have been used to describe Will 'o the Wisps and other natural luminescence. But also, in more modern lore as means for witches to recognise one another, in a kind of inner glow.

Reclaiming Magic

Magical practices are, for many people, archaic and strange, but for some, they are a part of everyday life, much as they were for our ancestors. Magic is somehow both familiar and new; human memories for millennia were based in a magical world. And perhaps it can take us on a voyage into the older, wilder, more primitive parts of the brain or thought, into the hidden depths of the unconscious, spirit, and the realms of human imagination and dream. Magic means different things to different people; it is a path that meanders past and through all those things that are just on the edges of healing, religion and science – magic is the unexpected, the exciting – that which takes us out of our ordinary state of consciousness and into some other, older, deeper, wilder place. Magic implies wildness and wonder, the archaic, mysterious and inexplicable. Synchronicity, a sense of spiritual connection, intuition – these are experiences that some people have all of the time, some may have experienced rarely, and a few never experience at all. Magic encompasses that whole in-between realm of experiences.

So, if the idea of magic interests you, I propose leaving a space for the unknown and unexplainable in the wild and being open to the magical and untamed. A space to let the possibility of magic in (or what our ancestors once called magic, you can name how you like – wonder, enchantment, awe). And to find that magic, we must begin in the wild places.

Let's Wander and Wonder...

The role of woodlands in most of our daily lives has been in decline for centuries. One might suggest we no longer understand the woods in the same way as our rural ancestors, but the wildwood still draws our imaginations, and offers new mysteries, even when viewed from the bright lights of our expanding cities or accessed via high-speed roads. After generations of deforestation and decline woodlands are being valued once more. The woods which once inspired folktales, songs, books and art, are finding new uses in healthcare, rewilding and community projects and as outdoor classrooms for children and adults. The ever-changing wildwoods still have the power to transform and sustain us, literally and metaphorically.

And so, if I have piqued your interest, put on your walking boots and pack your rucksack. There is no singular path for any of this. Stories and beliefs are revived and changed over time, witches are seen and talked of in a hundred different ways, and the origins of words and customs are all a winding forest pathway with many forks and fallen leaves that obscure the way. Perhaps these fairy stories, folk tales and legends will lay bare some of the sources of our fears as well as what the wildwood can mean in terms of transformation and healing, how the wild environs can reflect our own wildness, and how we might reclaim this. The witch, who features so prevalently, seems to be intertwined with the wood and wild, like creeping vines and earthen roots. We may find her bones buried within tree trunks or her charms hung from branches; we may hear her stories of fated whispers and journeys with root-cutters and cunning folk foraging for medicines. The witch is ever present in the wildwood – this book will explore just some of the ways this is true.

Let us journey into wild possibility and, with the help of the witch, explore the wonders of the wildwood. Let us risk getting lost as we gather a wise story or two to hold onto as we walk into the darkest hearts of the woods; we are going to need them, to remind us of what can lead us to lose our way. The witch seems to live and thrive where we may fear to tread. Asks us to leave the comfort of our hearth fires and walk into the wild and the wood. So, come to the trees, my love; there is magic here so ancient, so vast, you can barely imagine...

I

INTO THE WOODS

I t is a curious thing how a walk through the trees can awaken the senses and challenge our imaginations. Every tree holds secrets, in ring upon circling ring. And to enter the world of trees is to enter into nature's magic. These ancient beings watch the hustle and bustle of the world from their steady spot, their roots reaching into the memory of the land, illustrating growth and change with every season. The forest remembers, stories of drought and fire, healing and hardships, information never entirely lost for those who know how to read the trees. The forest is like a library, an archive.

Throughout human history, plants, trees, herbs and flowers have been symbols for beliefs and religions, fears and superstitions. In mythology, trees, their blossoms and fruit, become symbols of gods and deities, for seasons of the year, as well as treasured for their medicinal and nutritious properties. Almost all trees seem to hold overlapping qualities of being considered protective guardians, and gateways to other realms as they connect to the lower worlds via their roots and up to the heavenly sky through their branches.

There have been cultures and points in history when the partnership of human and earth was deeply honoured, where offerings were given and gratitude habitually shared, and prayers were made in sacred groves.

From the early ages of humankind, trees and the woods that hold them have been associated with both natural and otherworldly forces that should be respected. Trees represent so many things to us as humans: nourishment for both body and spirit, transformation, time passing, growth, union and fertility. They are the places of birth, life and death, sacred shrines and sites of pilgrimage, ritual, ceremony and celebration. Certain trees have a place in mythology, folklore and magic because they have always, in vast-ranging cultures, been seen (quite rightly) as sacred and valuable. Sacred trees are found in Hindu, Aboriginal, Egyptian, Sumerian, Norse, Japanese, Buddhist, Christian and Celtic traditions (to name just a few).

TREE TALES: ASH (FRAXINUS EXCELSIOR)

"In the old times, when people were more ready to see and believe strange things than they are now, when magic powers were thought possible, and every poor old woman was supposed to be a witch, the ash tree belonged to the world of mystery and possessed wonderful gifts."

Mrs Dyson, *The Stories of the Trees* (1896)

To those that work with them today ash wands are used in healing magic, and a popular construction of modern witch's brooms is an ash staff with birch twigs and a willow binding.

Ash in the house was considered a charm of protection from witchcraft or malefic magic, a staff of ash over the door guarded the entrance from evil influences. However "ash trees were not planted close to the house or crops, because their vigorous root system can damage stonewalls or hinder the growth of crops."[1]

In Hampshire, UK, magic rituals would take place where a child was passed through the split trunk of an ash tree as a cure for broken or weak limbs. And ash sap may be given to newborns for protection from "witches, fairies, and other imps of darkness."[2]

Like many trees Ash has its own protector in folk tales and superstitions – in Scandinavia and Germany, it is the Ash Wife or Ash Woman – Askafroa or Eschenfrau who is the spirit who lives inside the ash tree. She is a fierce guardian of the ash trees, so ferocious as to be considered to be something of a demon. She was honoured with offerings of beer or milk to keep her amenable.

A Magical Life

Following the end of the last Ice Age (some ten thousand years ago), much of Europe grew into a natural wooded landscape, within which lived elk, reindeer, bear, bison, wolves, wild cats, as well as insects and plants. Ancient woodland was diverse and included many trees; oak, ash, yew, beech, birch, hazel, holly to name just a few. Britain, which is where, for me, this story begins – was never covered completely in woodland; more of a patchwork of woods, alongside pastureland, grass, marsh, moor and meadow, chalk downs and vast swathes of royal hunting forests – the trees that have survived are living links to our history.

As the human population grew, demands for food, fuel, shelter, grazing and growing land, increased. Slowly but surely, large areas were cleared. "Ancient woodland" is a term now used in the British Isles for the woods that remain from around the year 1600 – our remaining ancient woodland covers just 2.5-3% of the land.[3] That forest, full of the unknown as it was, was also where even the poorest soul might find shelter and food: mushrooms, nuts, berries, herbs, roots and wild game, 'need foods' and nourishment. In skilled hands these would also be turned into medicines and balms to cure and calm.

Life for rural people in ancient to early modern Europe (and many places beyond) was magical. Not in the way we might use the word today – but an awareness and responsiveness to unseen forces accepted as part of commonplace life. These forces swirled around the edges and dark corners not yet eroded by religion or science. For our ancestors, life was more precarious and mysterious. There was an accepted worldview of how and why things happened that included, but was not limited to, magic, demons, curses, bewitchment, evil eyes, charms and warding.

For our ancestors, life was a dance with unseen forces, a constant interaction with the magical and unpredictable. Understanding and appeasing these forces was essential for protection, survival, and finding meaning in a world that often seemed beyond human control. The wildwoods, the undomesticated and mysterious places, were integral to this magical worldview. They were home to nature spirits, magical beings and deities, and journeys into these wild spaces held significant importance for rituals and pilgrimage.

In the past, magic was part of understanding and interpreting uncertainties and insecurities; magic offered reassuring actions to take. For example, to interpret the world as governed by specific nature spirits instead of an abstract 'nature' gave a face and name to mysterious forces of nature, made them slightly less fearful perhaps, and offered a way to find meaning (where meaning may or may not be truly present). To understand these spirits, stories would be told about them, and actions could be taken to appease them, such as charms and offerings, or their dwelling places could be avoided. Stories gave a symbolic structure to the world, such as dividing it into cultivated places: cities, towns and farmlands, and wild places: hills, forests and lakes. And so, these wild places often became the haunt of spirits, magical beings and deities. Journeys to wild spaces might be part of magical rituals or pilgrimage (or rituals in the home may intend, instead, to keep those of the wild spaces at bay).

Early pagan* beliefs held such strong reverence for trees: as sacred beings, as resources for feeding, healing, fuel and sources of wisdom, that early Christian crusaders throughout Europe cut down sacred trees and groves, literally toppling old idols and old gods, and in some cases, building churches over the remains. The most sacred of pagan places were transformed into the most unholy in Christian eyes, and the souls that worshipped at earth's altar became witches, demons and heathens.

---

* Celt, heathen and pagan were all words created to describe the rural folks of Britain and Europe. Celt meaning barbarian – a tribal peoples, not belonging to one of the prominent civilisations: Greek, Roman, Christian. And a term later used in the Middle Ages was 'peasant'. None of these groups was completely 'wild', but they were often considered so by city folks and those who saw themselves as the more civilised party.

Disenchantment

The fall of humanity from our initial state of grace, according to the Bible, was due to the first woman eating from the Tree of Knowledge. Because of her wickedness, humanity was punished evermore. The domination of European lands by Christianity led to beliefs in the inherent evil of wild nature and man's duty to bend the land and its creatures to his will. These spiritual beliefs became the underpinnings of Western law and culture.

The slow transition to industrial capitalism and the rise of rationalism led to disenchantment on many levels. Communal fields were hedged and fenced off, woodlands cleared, wild lands tamed and made productive, old boundaries disappeared and populations displaced from their rural lives. This was accomplished over centuries, through successive Enclosures laws from 1604 to 1914 and massive industrialisation and urbanisation. This is all part of the story of the gradual detachment of human societies from the natural world and the devaluing and dehumanising of people in the transition to capitalism. This power shift also bought us to a view that we largely still hold today: that labour which earns a wage is seen as the only work of worth, in contrast, for example, to 'invisible labour'. Unpaid caring work, the birthing of children, home crafts, wildcrafts, foraging was not now seen as valuable (and to many still isn't).

> *"In this sense, we have to think of the enclosures as a broader phenomenon than simply the fencing off of land. We must think of an enclosure of knowledge, of our bodies, and of our relationship to other people and nature."*

Silvia Frederici, *Witches, Witch-hunting, and Women* (2018)

This is a complex history, and certainly, people migrated from the country to the city for many reasons, but this is a noteworthy point in the story, as less and less wild and wooded land was accessible by common folk, and more and more being owned and fenced off by large wealthy landowners. This loss of common land brought scarcity for many common people, and perhaps you might imagine the old woman who lives alone in her tumbledown cottage covered in ivy, no longer able to graze her pigs, unable to work, she must rely on charity, but she is not well-liked because she is cranky and argumentative so is given no assistance from her neighbours. Perhaps she swears or curses them in frustration, and if at any point after this a cow falls ill or weather blights crops…soon enough she is accused of being a witch (again, by no means is this the only reason accusations happened, but you can see how the stories can intertwine).

A Rekindling

There was a significant jump in urbanisation over the course of a century, from the beginning of the 1800s, when about 80% of English people lived in the countryside, to the early 1900s, when about 80% lived in towns and cities. This was a pattern replicated across the Western world. As much as cities could improve certain aspects of life, there was a collective longing for the simplicity, beauty and freedom of rural life. The collective idea of a rural idyll of healthy and strong country folk, full of wisdom for the land and rich with generations of passed down knowledge and skill was a comforting thought, recalled in story and song. Even as urbanization and modernization changed the landscape and the fortunes of many, the allure of the wild persisted, and the nostalgia for the rural idyll grew as an increasingly urban population yearned for what they considered the simple rural life of their ancestors, working with nature's bounty rather than drudging for a wage.

And this yearning to connect with nature and reclaim ancient traditions became a guiding force for some people, including modern pagans and witches, as well as creatives such as poets and writers.

Tales and fables have been written down for as long as humans have been writing. But our journey to collecting and celebrating what we now call folklore and fairy tales really ignited through the 1600s into the 1800s (and beyond), as the popularity of folklore societies rose alongside the emergence of fairy tale collectors across Europe. Driven by elements including the Romantic movement's emphasis on the mystical and the past, as well as a growing interest in preserving and understanding national identities, scholars and enthusiasts flocked to document the rich oral traditions, myths and legends that had been passed down through generations, preserving and exploring cultural narratives.

From France, in the 1600s, prolific writer Marie-Catherine d'Aulnoy published a collection of stories titled *Les Contes des Fées (Tales of the Fairies,* 1697) and the term "fairy tale" was born. D'Aulnoy's tales often featured strong and resourceful female protagonists, reflecting her own perspective as a woman in a society dominated by male authors. In the same year – 1697 – Charles Perrault published *Tales and Stories of the Past with Morals (or Tales of Mother Goose)*. Later, another French storyteller, Gabrielle-Suzanne Barbot de Villeneuve was the first, in 1740, to write of the tale we now call "Beauty and the Beast" – where 'Beauty' finds herself prisoner in the castle of an angry Beast deep in the forest. Like D'Aulnoy, Villeneuve used her stories to comment on social and political issues of the time – this was essentially a cautionary tale for little girls, who, in this era of arranged marriages, were often forced into marrying older wealthy men, or men not of their choosing – they may well have to marry someone they considered a 'beast', but with love, and the valued traditional feminine niceties of patience, kindness and demureness (as Beauty portrays in the tale), he may become more of a man (sadly this wasn't always the case in real life). Fairy tales reflected the communities creating them, from those who grew up in fields, woods and forests to those who grew up in finishing schools and parlours.

From Germany, the collected *Children's and Household Tales* of

Jacob and Wilhelm Grimm's published in 1812, brought together a vast collection of German folktales. Danish Hans Christian Anderson similarly offered hundreds of tales over his career, starting with *Tales Told for Children* (1835). And in England, Joseph Jacobs collected and published a wide range of English fairy tales and folklore, such as *English Fairy Tales* (1890).

These tales were told for entertainment, for adults as much as for children – as we see in stories with deeper meanings such as "Beauty and the Beast". These tales were told to children, but nevertheless regularly had themes of infanticide, poverty, abuse and cannibalism. We are often told the 'nicer' versions in the present day (such as via the work of Disney), and some more frightening folk tales may be 'softened' to create more whimsical tales. But the stories also introduce children to very important ideas of what cruelty and hatred may lead someone to do, as well as the virtues of kindness, respect and the reward inherent in those, and morals that support lessons we hold for the rest of our lives. As adults, we may find within these stories, new meanings and ways through which we can explore emotions, life events and uncertainty.

The whispers of truth within these tales often spoke to real-life struggles, and here folklore, history and fairy tale meet just as witches existed in all three spheres, as did cruelty, hunger and fear of the unknown. This would have made them more fascinating and relevant to the lives of those reading and telling the tales and aided their longevity.

Many city dwellers did (and do) romanticise 'old ways' and the rural lifestyle (not necessarily a negative) because of that massive urban jump from 1800 to 1900. Pagan practices became the activities of a time past, offering visions of a life filled with communal festivals and social harmony, living close to nature, and more informed by wisdom of the natural world. Whilst the idealisation of the rural way of living as something of an aspiration or fantasy, was certainly the case for many, exploring and celebrating folk customs for clues to earlier cultures and British heritage is a valued endeavour. The Folklore Society was founded in London 1878, to do just this, where scholars, anthropologists, adventurers, and storytellers such as Barbara Aitken, Margaret Murray, Katharine Briggs, Julia Somerset and many others (I'm just naming a few of my personal favourites) wrote of regional folklore, witches, fairies and green men.

At the very least, this history reminds us that there are other ways of living, of being, and of finding joy – it hasn't always been this way. And whilst we can't go back, we can remember as we move forward.

The rise of folklore societies and fairy tale collectors in Europe left a lasting mark on cultural preservation and literary creation. And The Folklore Society continues today with awards, scholarships and events, as well as wider offerings of workshops on storytelling, online lectures on folklore and podcasts, all continuing this rich tradition of sharing and passing on tales.

LITTLE GOLDEN HOOD

"Le Petit Chaperon Rouge" by Charles Perrault (1697) became the "Little Red Riding Hood" story most of us are familiar with, but even earlier versions from rural France and Italy date all the way back to the eleventh century. However, in 1888 a French author called Charles Marelles wrote a version of the tale where the main character's red riding hood is replaced by a golden one. And shortly after, Andrew Lang would publish an English version in The Red Fairy Book (1890).

This is that alternative version of the girl in the riding hood, and her grandmother. I prefer this golden hooded version. In the familiar tale of "Little Red Riding Hood", the wolf deceived and devoured the girl along with her grandmother. In "Little Golden Hood", it was not she nor the good granddame but the wicked wolf who was caught and devoured. And no help from a woodcutter was needed! The story begins, perhaps in a familiar way...

There was once a little peasant girl, her name was Blanchette, but she was known as Little Golden Hood, on account of the cloak she wore, gold and fire coloured. It was given to her by her grandmother for good luck she said, for it was made of a ray of sunshine. And her Grandmother was one to be listened to. For she was so old that she did not know her age, and she was considered something of a witch, and everyone thought the little hood rather bewitched with her magic.

And so it was, as you will see.

One day little Golden Hood was tasked to take a good piece of cake to her grandmother in the next village, and there was a wildwood to cross before getting there. Golden Hood set forth along the woodland path, but at a turn, suddenly, a wolf appeared. He had seen the child start out alone, and this villain was waiting to devour her, but he approached her as a friend.

"Where are you going, my pretty one?"

"I am going to my grandmother's house on the other side of the woods," she replied.

The wolf wished Golden Hood a fair journey and passed her by. But in shadows he cut through the trees apace and arrived at the grandmother's house in just minutes. He knocked at the door, but there was no answer. The old woman had risen early to sell healing herbs in the town, and the wolf had a notion. Creeping into the house, he pulled on grandmother's night-cap down to his eyes, and then he lay down in the bed.

In this time, Blanchette had journeyed quietly on her way, picking wildflowers, watching the little birds making their nests, and butterflies which fluttered in the sunshine. And when at last she arrived at the little house – in she walked. And she was much surprised:

"Grandmother!" she exclaimed, "What hairy arms you've got!"

"All the better to hug you, dear child," the wolf replied.

"What a big tongue you've got!"

"All the better for answering, dear child."

"And what great white teeth you have!"

"All the better for devouring little children!" the wolf replied and bared his teeth to devour Blanchette.

But the girl ducked down so quickly that the wolf caught only her little hood on his teeth. He drew back, shaking his jaw in pain: the little fire-coloured hood had burnt him. The little hood, you see, was indeed magical, just as rumours said. So now the wolf, burnt and howling, made a leap to the door to escape. But at this exact moment, Grandmother arrived, returning from the town with her sack of herbs now empty on her shoulder. She caught the wolf in her sack and emptied it into her well, where the wolf, still howling, tumbled in and drowned.

"Well!" Grandmother exclaimed, just a little out of breath, "without my little magic golden hood, where would you be, my darling?"

Blanchette promised to keep it with her always for protection. And, to restore their hearts after such an adventure, they sat down by the hearth and enjoyed a large piece of cake each and a good draught of golden wine.

It is said that you may still see Little Golden Hood dancing through woods and wild meadows, but you must rise very early on a sunny day, and you may catch a glimpse of her magic hood shining under the first warm golden rays of the morning.

Fairy Tale

"The stories and lessons within fairy tales are often blends of elements of classic legends and ancient mythology, recounted over generations, evolving into amalgamations of morality tales with the same features: the witch in the forest; the hero's quest; battles of good versus evil."

Sarah Robinson, *Kitchen Witch: Food, Folklore & Fairy Tale* (2022)

Fairy tales, superstition and folktales continue to fascinate us (amongst many other reasons) because they work in a kind of liminal space. The folklore and superstitions surrounding the wildwoods in these stories are on a spectrum: will an acorn in your pocket protect you from lightning? Probably not. Will wild mint or willow bark have a physiological effect on your body? Yes, absolutely. Finding golden treasures within a tree or in its branches – well, yes, although it won't be golden coins! Seeing messages or portents in the dancing leaves or sacred groves, to some skilled people, yes, that's a reality. And trees are a place where nourishment can be gathered and put into cauldrons, whether that be the brew of the wood wives, forager or rural cook, the knowledge inspired by deities or the handed-down knowledge of simple herbal remedies. There's magic to be found if you look carefully enough…

The woods are one of the most common fairy tale settings: "Hansel and Gretel", "Snow White", "Vasilissa the Beautiful", "Goldilocks and the Three Bears", "Little Red Riding Hood" to name just a few of the best-known tales, are all set in the woods. The wildwood is an enchanting, liminal space, outside of the security and familiarity of the town. But the woods are not just a scenic background; they possess a living presence that weaves itself into the very fabric of the tales – it is a presence that embodies the themes of the tales themselves, functioning under its own set of rules, its own wild magic.

Fairy tales may well be our first experience of the deep dark centre of ancient woods and mythical wilds. We may uncover the threads of archetypes woven through narratives, reminding us that within every forest lies both the potential for trepidation and the promise of revelation. These timeless stories beckon us to venture beyond the safety of the known and step into the wilds of the unknown. By doing so, we embrace the mysteries that lie within ourselves and within the world around us. In the realm of witches and wildwoods, we find not only the allure of magical beings but also the reflection of our own hidden desires, fears and aspirations.

HANSEL AND GRETEL

A shortened version of the fairy tale that features in Volume 1 of Children's and Household Tales *by The Brothers Grimm (1812).*

One of the functions of fairy tales is as cautionary tales for children, urging them not to stray from the path, eat strange things or trust strangers, and offering terrifying consequences of what might befall them if they do. They also try to cultivate qualities such as obedience, respect, discernment, self-reliance, having the courage to speak up and planning ahead. Such tales often spoke to real-life struggles, and here in "Hansel and Gretel" folklore, history and fairy tale meet, weaving the fates of cruel parents, starving children and strangers in woods, speaking to our hunger, fear of poverty and desire for pleasure and safety, timeless themes which give the stories longevity.

A poor woodcutter and his wife lived on the edge of a large forest. He could barely provide the daily bread for his wife and two children, Hansel and Gretel. One night his wife said to him, "We must take the children into the middle of the forest and leave them there. We can no longer feed them, if we don't, we shall all starve."

The children, still awake, heard everything that their mother said. Gretel began to cry. But Hansel whispered, "Don't cry. I'll find a way to help us," and he got up and crept outside. Under the moonlight, he gathered as many white pebbles from the ground as he could. Early the next morning, before sunrise, they set out.

When they reached the heart of the forest, they lit a fire. Their mother said, "Now, children, rest by the fire, we're going into the forest to gather wood. We'll come back and get you."

Hansel and Gretel sat by the fire waiting for their mother and father to return. Night fell, and the full moon rose, Hansel took Gretel by the hand. The pebbles glittered like silver coins and showed them the way home. They walked the whole night long and were back at their house by dawn.

Their father rejoiced when he saw his children again. But not long after this, there was, once again, nothing to eat in the house. And come dawn, once more, they found themselves walking into the forest. All Hansel had this time was a little bread, which he scattered on the ground as he had the pebbles. The children were led even deeper into the forest, and once again, they were to sleep by the fire, and once again, their parents did not return. Gretel shared her bread with Hansel because he had dropped his along the path.

When the moon rose, Hansel looked for the breadcrumbs. But they were gone. The birds had gobbled them up. The children soon lost their way amongst the trees, walking all night and all day until they fell asleep from exhaustion. They were now also very hungry. But as luck would have it, they came to a little house made of bread, with cake for roof tiles and clear sugar panes for windows.

Hansel had eaten a good piece of roof, and Gretel had devoured several small round windows before they heard a shrill voice cry from inside: "Nibble, Nibble, I hear a mouse! Who's that nibbling on my house?" Hansel and Gretel were so frightened they dropped their handfuls of the house.

A small, old woman appeared at the door. "Well now, dear children, where did you come from? Come inside with me." She made them a meal of milk and pancakes with sweet fruits and nuts. Afterwards, she made up two soft beds, and Hansel and Gretel thought themselves in heaven. The hag, however, was really a wicked witch. She had built the house only to lure children to her so she could kill, cook and eat them. It would be a happy feast day for her.

Early the next morning, she grabbed Hansel and stuck him into a cage. She shook Gretel and sent her to fetch water and cook breakfast, so that they may fatten up Hansel for eating. Frightened, Gretel did as the witch demanded.

Time passed, and one evening the witch declared today would be the day that Hansel would be cooked. But first they would bake some bread, a nice fresh loaf to accompany the main course. The old woman's eyes were weak, so she called Gretel over to see if the bread was cooked. "Sit down on the board," she said, "and I'll push you inside so that you can look properly."

The witch planned to trap Gretel inside, to bake and eat her too, of course. But Gretel was clever and said, "Show me how. Sit down on the board, and I'll shove you inside." And as the old woman sat on the board, Gretel shoved her inside as far as she could and shut the oven door and bolted it shut. The old woman screamed in the hot oven, and Gretel ran off and freed Hansel as the witch burned to death.

They filled their pockets with sweets and valuables from the cottage and found their way home. Their father rejoiced to see them again. His wife had died, and apparently, he hadn't spent a single happy day since his children had been away. Now he was a rich man.

Real and Fictional Woods

"Our myths, our legends, aren't necessarily true, but they are truly necessary. They have to do with the way we interpret the world and our place in it."

Jo Walton, *What Makes This Book So Great: Re-reading the Classics of Science Fiction and Fantasy* (2014)

When we hear the names of certain woodlands – Narnia, Lothlórien and Mirkwood for example – vivid images probably spring to mind. These are fictional woodlands but very real in their presence within our thoughts and memories. Mirkwood and Lothlórien are both fictional realms in J.R.R. Tolkien's Middle Earth.* Mirkwood is a term Tolkien uses to describe dark and foreboding forests, often inhabited by hostile creatures, and a symbol of decay and dark magic. In contrast, Lothlórien is a golden-hued enchanted forest located to the east (where the sun rises), it is a place of ethereal, serene beauty, and graceful elven inhabitants. In the enchanting world of Narnia, a wondrous snowy wood lies concealed beyond the confines of a wardrobe. Here, a malevolent White Witch wields such formidable power that she shrouds the entire land in an eternal winter, holding off the promise of Christmas and the Christ metaphor – Aslan the lion – with her power.

Other woodlands that hold a place in many hearts – Sherwood Forest, Pendle Forest, The Black Forest and Great Birnam Wood† – are all-too-real woodlands, used as settings for characters that blur between the folkloric and the historical. These woods have witnessed the passage of time and may have been home to remarkable figures like Robin Hood, adding depth to their history. In Shakespeare's

---

* Other authors have used the term Mirkwood but I would wager Tolkien's is the most well-known by some way.

† Sadly, just two trees remain of the great Birnam Wood of Shakespeare's time; the Birnam Oak and the Birnam Sycamore.

Macbeth, the witches known as the wyrd sisters make a prophecy that Macbeth will be vanquished when Great Birnam Wood moves to Dunsinane Hill, which leads Macbeth to believe that he is invincible because how could a forest possibly move? However, the prophecy comes to pass as soldiers cut branches from Birnam Wood to use as camouflage, effectively making the wood walk towards Dunsinane Hill and Macbeth is killed – as foretold by the witches. In the enchanted woods nothing is impossible.

In the enchanting realm of literature, real woods and fictional woods stand side by side as captivating settings that play a role in weaving tales of wonder and adventure, like A.A. Milne's Hundred Acre Wood, based on Ashdown Forest in Sussex, UK, whilst the main character is based on a real boy, Christopher Robin, and his toy bear, Winnie the Pooh, it is inhabited by imaginary talking animals. It's a wild and wonderful blend. Every point on the spectrum is covered.

Legends and folklore surrounding real woods demonstrate the profound connection humans have had with the natural world, shaping cultural beliefs and practices. In contrast, fictional woods allow authors to delve into the depths of their creativity, creating symbolic landscapes that can mirror aspects of our own world.

Though our modern ways of storytelling – through film, audiobook, ebook and podcast accessed on smartphones and tablets – would seem like magic to our ancestors, still the old themes of the witch and the wildwood continue to captivate us. She has been brought into modern folklore in horror movies like *The Blair Witch Project* (1999) and *The Witch* (2015), and classics are continually reimagined such as *Gretel & Hansel* (2020), *Into the Woods* (2014), *Tangled* (2010) and *Once Upon a Time* (2011) and big movie franchises such as the Marvel and Star Wars universes, to name just a fraction. The presence of a dark forest, a place tied to witchcraft in many cultures, highlights conflict between the civilised world and the wild natural world, just as it has been in centuries of folk tales. Forests are associated with monsters, which may be met in the wilderness where one may find liberation or be consumed by the wild.

Some of the woods we tell stories of are real, some are entirely fictional, and some reside somewhere in between – the same as the witch. The power of the human imagination and every myth and story imbues any place with magic. What is real? What is fiction? Where is the line? The wildwoods manage to embody a fusion of both real and fictional elements beyond the confines of a single narrative, intertwining real history with mythical creatures and fantastical adventures. The wildwoods can serve as a boundless canvas where authors, artists and storytellers can explore timeless themes.

2

THE WITCH OF
THE WILDWOOD IN
FOLKLORE & FAIRYTALE

"The woods are chaotic and wild; life goes on unseen within them, and for every lovely globe flower, springing golden in a small patch in sunshine, there is a death cap – Amanita phalloides – shiny, olive and yellow, just as pretty, but deadly poisonous, lurking under the oak trees. And in the stories, for every kindly old woman who gives you a useful gift, there is a very similar one who may gobble you up, put you under an enchantment or imprison you in a tower."

Sara Maitland, *Gossip from the Forest: The Tangled Roots of Our Forests and Fairytales* (2013)

Stories of the witch of the gingerbread house deep in the heart of the forest, the sorceress waiting in the trees for travellers to stray from the path, or the poor woman gathering sticks and herbs to sell at market, these classic fairy tales are woven deeply into our shared memories. A large part of our ideas and superstition of the witch in the woods are drawn from the fact that for many of us as children our first glimpse of the witch is through fairy stories – and she is very often in the woods – and so even as adults we can't help but envisage the witch in a woodland setting, perhaps holding a shining apple, or beside her little hut, beckoning us in…

Fairy tales that unfold in the woods offer us a unique perspective on the witch and the wildwoods. In fairy tale the witch is often a complex or ambiguous figure, not just a villain but a keeper of ancient wisdom, protector of hidden spaces, the embodiment of the woods' enchantment. The witch represents many things that stand just a little way beyond our understanding. She stands at the edges of 'manmade' places we consider safer than the wilds, the last human waymarkers before the land of streetlights tumbles away to moss, leaf, bark and the creaking of ancient boughs. These witches and women-like figures may evoke fears, but they are also guardians of long-forgotten words and songs, keepers of rituals of earth goddesses, fairy folk and nature spirits, and unseelie and unsettling histories.

Folklore warns and whispers of female forms that dwell deep in the forest. Sometimes a witch or other magical figure personifies the power of this dark, natural world to both terrify and mystify. Each witch of the woods has her own unique skills, quirks and personality. And stories may allow one to face fears and learn about the wildwood's many faces, wisdom, and power.

Within these tales lies the opportunity to confront and explore the many facets of the wisdom and power of women and wild souls. The stories of witches are not merely cautionary, they offer a chance to glimpse ideas of strength and resilience and connection to the earth. The witch may stand as a guardian of ancient knowledge, preserving the rituals and traditions that honour the cycles of nature.

In the depths of the forest, the witch embodies the spirit of the wildwoods, weaving spells and stirring the cauldron of transformation, inviting us to look beyond the surface and embrace the mystery of the unknown.

So, as we peer into the shadows of the woods, let us not only be wary but curious. Let us seek to understand the witch's secrets and unravel the threads of her ancient wisdom. In doing so, we may discover the powerful truths hidden within the heart of the wildwoods and, perhaps, within ourselves.

THE GIRL WHO MET THE WITCH OF THE WOODS

From the Swedish fairy tale, various versions can be found, this is a short version of the one written by Helena Nyblom (1843-1926) – a contemporary of Hans Christian Anderson.

Like so many fairy tales, this is a story of the innocent child going out into the wild – the good child who should show faith, obedience and temperance and "take the straight road" in order to stay safe. Danger is portrayed through the character of the witch: she is both catalyst for change and corruptor. The witch represents many negative traits (for good Christian women): greed, pride, power, selfishness, willfulness. She doesn't give birth like a 'good' woman should, but rather steals her children.

Once, there was an old charcoal burner who lived on a mountainside with his wife and their little daughter Maria. Their humble cottage sat on the edge of a big wild forest and deep in this forest was the kiln where the wood was burned for charcoal. One day, her mother asked Maria to take a jug of sweet milk to her grandmother. She warned Maria to take the straight road through the forest and not to take any shortcuts through the trees – for one could lose their way in the wild forest. Maria set off with her little milk jug and soon was deep into the forest. She knew the way to grandma's well – it was straight ahead thought the forest and then through a meadow. Grandma's little cottage sat between the birch trees and the mountain ash.

It was a beautiful midsummer evening, the sun shone through the trees and the forest was in full midsummer bloom with birch and alder leaves spreading lush green canopies, twinflowers and lingonberry were blooming and the pine resin glistened in the sun like gems and smelled wonderful. Maria was feeling very happy and sang a little song her father taught her as she walked:

Don't waste your time in the tavern,

Don't lose your way in the wood.

Only be faithful,

Always be faithful,

And your corn will grow ripe and good.

But as she sang, a long green shadow crossed beside her in the trees. Closer and closer the green shadow came, and lo, it was not a shadow at all but a tall woman wearing a green cape and green hat. Maria did not know it, but this was the Witch of the Woods. She cackled and made a sound like a mountain stream crashing over pebbles – and it sent a chill through little Maria.

The witch had a round white face and fluttering red-gold

hair. Her eyes were the lightest of blues, like a spring sky, but shaped like a cat's. Her mouth was red like lingonberries and her teeth were sharp and pointed.

"I know the quickest path to take," said the witch. "You don't know the forest like I do, you'll not find a better guide than me!" And before she knew what was happening, the witch had taken Maria's hand and marched onto a narrow forest path.

The evening sun was low now and burned through the dark mountain pines. The witch showed Maria sweet wild strawberries which she ate – they were delicious. Then she showed her thousands of lilies of the valley which were growing among young white trunked birches. Surrounded by the sweet scent Maria felt drowsy. Now it was the witch who sang as she walked:

Deep in the forest I shall hide you,

Long, long, until you are lost.

For I weave pine needles, and hide my path,

I scatter witch herbs at roads' cross.

The pine forest grew even thicker, and the evening light was fading fast. They came to a steep mountain wall where the witch drew her finger against the stone and it cracked open. She carried Maria into the mountain before the crack closed behind them. The witch laid Maria on a bed of moss and they both slept.

Come morning the witch took Maria out into the forest once more. "Now you are mine, I will show you my kingdom," the witch said, and they ran through the forest together. The witch could leap like a hare, float like a dragonfly over marshes and wriggle under thick bushes like a snake. And Maria could now do the same. They flew to the top of the pine trees and could see for miles over woods and mountains.

"I will live for a long time," said the witch, "until this green earth disappears – who knows how long that will be. But I shall have fun until that time!"

And so the summer went by, day by day. They jumped through mountain waters and sailed on logs and swung on trees in the storms. The witch scared peasants travelling through the woods – she shrieked as if all the wild animals of the forest had shrieked at once. "Here comes the Queen of the forest, out of my way!" the witch would call to animals and people alike.

Maria followed her everywhere, her memory lost in this place. She was enchanted by the witch and her songs, the mysteries of the forest and the wild waterfalls were in her songs. But so were sadness and fury.

Autumn came, hazel bushes held ripe brown nuts in sunny groves and the pair feasted on nuts. The mountain ash were full of blood-red berries, birds set to their migrations and dead leaves danced on the forest floor. The witch and Maria watched the villagers harvest the fields of golden corn.

In the harvesting fields they saw a peasant woman had left her infant wrapped by the side of the field while she worked. The witch bade Maria to take the infant. But this request was so terrible, that the spell over Maria slipped for a moment and Maria saw now, the cruelty of the witch. She refused to take the child. The witch was so furious that she left Maria in the fields.

As evening grew near, the witch had to return to the mountain, for she feared the stars. Maria stayed in the fields as the sun set. The witch shrieked and retreated into her mountain. This was Maria's chance to be free! And she ran as fast as her feet would carry her. Far, far she travelled and she was tired and weary, but she willed herself on, and she was singing a long-forgotten song to keep her spirits up as she passed a very elderly couple pulling a cart behind them.

Don't waste your time in the tavern,

Don't lose your way in the wood.

Only be faithful,

Always be faithful,

And your corn will grow ripe and good.

The old man gasped for he recognised the song as one that he had once, long ago taught his daughter. He looked at her and wept. The old woman threw her arms around her neck, "My poor darling child, it has been ten years since you left home to carry milk to your grandma, we feared the Witch of the Woods had claimed you and know we know it to be true."

Maria sat with them and wept, for all the time they had lost, and for her grandma, now dead, who never got her milk...

ANCIENT WISE ONES

"A witch ought never to be frightened in the darkest forest [...] because she should be sure in her soul that the most terrifying thing in the forest was her."

Terry Pratchett, *Wintersmith* (2008)

Some of the witches of the woods could be considered the ancient wise ones of the woods in human guise, others were folk forced into hiding, some were an early incarnation of what we might now call a herbalist, midwife or healer, others were just called old or grandmother, women who lived their own way on the fringes of society. Their stories have been rewritten many times. The many faces of these 'witches' were formed and reformed by each society that envisioned them.

From worshipping old gods beneath the gleaming moon to druids sacrificing to the oak tree, to a fairy tale hag gripping a broom by her tumbledown cottage and stroking her familiar,* many witches, magic makers and magical beings seem bound to the forest. A wildwood dwelling may contain a wicked witch you desperately seek to escape (like in the Grimms' fairy tale "Hansel and Gretel"), or you may meet an old woman who will save you both (like in the Grimms' fairy tale "The Robber Bridegroom") or one that blends the line between terrifying hag and wise helper, like Baba Yaga, from *Old Russian Tales.*

The witch is endlessly fascinating (and demonised) as a scapegoat to befallings of misfortune. From illness to weather, nightmares to mania, crop blights and stolen butter have, in certain places and in certain times, been blamed upon the witch. And because the witch will often guide us to many kindred spirits in the eyes of superstitions, we'll also find fairies, spirits, trolls, goblins, devils, demons and restless ghosts. In the woods, we may meet both the delightful – the white stag, unicorn and flower fairy – and potentially terrifying – the outlaw, the wild folk, witch and wolves. In each culture, certain rituals and stories are unique (and tied together with common threads: fear of loss, for example), so when I explore the folklore of a place, I look to the witches. Those who hold a unique quality to exist in realms of history, folklore, superstition, fiction and the material world all at once.

Writers have been bewitched by magic workers since our first stories were committed to text (and I'm sure long before writing storytellers savoured these tales). Ancient texts feature stories of deities, demons and magical practices. The classical tales of Greece and Rome give us some of our first story witches of the western world: Circe – living in a palace isolated in the midst of a dense wood on her island of Aeaea, in company of lions and wolves; Medea with her

---

* A familiar was thought to be the cunning person's shapeshifting spirit helper, considered to be devilish in origin. At the height of the witch craze, even the presence of an animal could lead to someone being accused of being a witch.

knowledge of herbs and potions and Witch-Goddess Hecate of dark underworld accompanied by dogs. These fictional sorceresses inhabited the margins of society, symbolising and personifying peripheries, edges and boundaries. These witches made a big impression and these stereotypes have persisted, with their characterisations still acting as outlines for the portrayal of witches today.

WITCHCRAFT AND TREELORE

Historical and folkloric stories speak of the connection between witches and woods: witches gathering under trees, creating wild ritual and riding on branches, stories play upon the atmosphere of secrecy and sorcery that forests can evoke. Artists and storytellers certainly fostered this as they seized up this idea that there is something just a little intangible, liminal, about trees and forests: energy, supernatural forces, that which cannot be measured but can perhaps be closer examined in the human imagination; where one may find roaming ghosts of fallen souls, magical beings in flight under the canopy, and, of course, there may be the witch who was banished from her community. In every weathered woodland tale, we uncover just a little more: ways of knowing that were (and are) guided by landscape, identity, place, spirituality, folklore and mythology. Myth and superstition are borne from the landscape, especially within the dark, tangled heart of the wood or forest, a location beyond where people normally tread, where strange things might occur, and strange beings might call home.

The presence of trees in historical images of witches' gatherings often indicated that they are not taking place somewhere civilised and orderly like a home or building. Witches' gatherings were often said to be outside and in wild woods and forests – therefore both the events and the people who attended were considered suspicious, unruly, wild and strange. The woods were a place, perhaps the only place, where it was possible to defy social norms, offering a freedom from social constraints. (Magical gatherings, both ancient and present day may meet at hidden, but well-defined spots for both privacy and sacred connections such as old oak trees deep in the woods, or ancient stone monuments upon windswept moors). The inaccessibility of these areas made them a place where meetings of all sorts may well have taken place away from prying eyes, but also, for those not present to easily project all the fears and suspicions that their imaginations could concoct. Those who never saw these gatherings usually imagined the worst.

TREE TALES: JUNIPER (JUNIPERUS COMMUNIS)

Juniper smoke has been (and still is) part of Celtic, Germanic, Slavic, and Baltic rituals. One may burn juniper wood for its highly aromatic smoke for ritual purification and, for those who worked with such skills, aiding clairvoyance and contact with the Otherworld. Particularly at festivals throughout the year, the smoke may be used for cleansing and casting out of witchcraft and other undesirable fears, such as to prevent the spread of disease. In Scotland, people would attempt to expel the disease and malefic magic by "saining" (burning of herbs and wood to create fragrant smoke) the house and occupants with the smoke; the house was then aired, and the occupants revived with a dram of whisky.

In Germany, the tree spirit or goddess of the juniper is *Frau Wacholder*, a personification and presiding spirit of the juniper. Her name echoes the tree's German name, *Wacholder* (from Old High German *wachal*, "awake"), because the tree has been perceived as a guardian on watch, acting as an intermediary between humankind and the spirit world. And in turn, Frau Wacholder is a sharp observer, she sees everything. And as such, she might be invoked for the return of stolen or lost things. In Germany, like in Scotland, juniper is believed to drive away spells and witchcraft from the homestead.

When Ulrich Molitor wrote *De Lamiis et phitonicis mulieribus* (literally: *Of the Lamias and the Pythoness women* – both descriptors of monstrous women/witches) in 1489 it was intended to explain the realities of witchcraft that could appeal to the general public, (and a slightly fairer, more nuanced exploration of witchcraft in contrast to the extreme, unhinged views of the *Malleus Maleficarum** published a few years earlier). The book was popular and reprinted in various iterations and was vividly illustrated (it was the first illustrated text on witchcraft and provided its readers with a visual image of witchcraft and those who allegedly practiced it). The book includes a woodcut of three women feasting by a tree, at first this image may look very normal, just three women eating...but this is what Molitor called "The Witches' Convivium" (what others would call a witches sabbath) and it is the tree that is the key, showing that the feasting is taking place in the natural world, outside of the domestic realm.

Similar imagery in more bawdy detail can be seen in Hans Baldung's *The Witches/Witches Sabbath* (1510) where naked women are blending potions, feasting, gesturing grandly and riding on goat back. A single tree in the foreground clarifies this is all happening in the 'wild', away from civilised society. Other examples include Agostino Veneziano's *The Witches' Procession (Lo Stregozzo)* or *The Carcass* (1520), where naked revellers ride amongst skeletal and demonic animals, through plants and swaying trees, and *Linda Maestra! (Pretty Teacher!)* by Francisco Goya (1799), which also features a

---

* The *Malleus* is so bonkers that it's become one of the most well-known historical texts on witches by virtue of the fact that it illustrates an extreme in terms of hatred of both witchcraft and women. Even at the time of writing its author was considered something of a crank with some severe fixations. But as the book travelled – and people who didn't know of Heinrich Kramer read it, like many ideas of superstitions and legend – the truth and myth got blurred and many took the book more seriously. Especially when it was printed with a 'papal bull' (a type of official document issued by the Pope) at the front, which leant it a gravitas it shouldn't have warranted. But even I must admit it features a very memorable tree-based story (and proof, if it was needed, that the entire book is full of nonsensical stories that had horrifying consequences for real women) which told of 'witches' that were fond of stealing men's penises and hiding them in trees, keeping them alive in bird's nests by feeding them oats.

single tree below two witches and an owl in flight. Artworks such as these examples contributed strongly to, and drew strongly from, superstition, and folk imagery of the witch as connected to the natural world and especially the tree in a perpetual cycle of influence.

In folklore and fairy tale, trees and women seem to have been feared for their ability and tendency to speak the truth. To say perhaps, that which some would not wish to hear. In several Russian fairy tales and some versions of "The Juniper Tree" by the Brothers Grimm, the tree itself utters the truth (often because of slain bodies amongst their roots). Trees are often symbols of truth, and of time, by which secrets are revealed. The witch is often unpopular for the same reason – for sharing, shouting and cackling a few uncomfortable facts, secrets or predictions of undesirable futures.

TREE TALES: ELDER (SAMBUCUS NIGRA)

The rosy orange sap of the elder tree fed the superstition that the elder tree would bleed if it was cut down, and that apologies should be made if cutting was attempted, lest one incur bad luck and wrath from all manner of beings who held the elder in high regard or dwelled within it. Inhabitants of the elder tree branches have included: witches, elves, fairies and the elder mother. An elder tree is among the many things that witches were thought able to transform themselves into, and in Ireland particularly, witches rode elder branches in the wind rather than besom broomsticks. They are also known to love to lurk beneath the shadow of its branches or within them...

"In Germany, the Elder is regarded with great respect... The pith of the branches, when cut in round flat shapes, is dipped in oil, lighted, and then put to float in a glass of water; its light on Christmas Eve is thought to reveal to the owner all the witches and sorcerers in the neighbourhood."

Richard Folkard, *Plant Lore, Legends, and Lyrics* (1884)

As with many trees, and within the wealth of tree folklore, we find contradictions of uses – so although connected to witches, the elder was also used as a protective charm against them: crosses made from elder wood were hung inside stables, doors and windows of the house to protect the inhabitants. Because it was connected to witches and wise women, people were very likely to use the elder in works of medicine or charms.

Travellers carried an elder twig to ward off thieves or ward off sickness, and elderberries collected on Midsummer's Eve* were said to save their possessor from witchcraft and awarded magic powers. All parts of the elder can be useful and powerful in healing, so perhaps these beliefs evolved to protect a valuable resource.

* Folk charms can speak of the magical properties of fruits and flowers that cannot actually be found at a certain time of year. In this case, in June, elders would still be in blossom, so finding a berry, would be such a rarity, if ever, one might see it as magical. Also, folk tales such as this may hint at the fact that one could never entirely protect oneself from the bad luck that may be attributed to witchcraft – and so appropriate charms were actually unattainable things – one may spend a lifetime seeking an elderberry that appeared in June, or a primrose that flowered at Midsummer (and many of us still look for 'lucky' four leaf clovers, although they are slightly more common...).

THE ELDER TREE WITCH

A folk tale from Somerset, England, found in Forgotten Folktales of the English Counties *by Ruth Tongue.*

Wise old grandmothers are not always cast as witches, sometimes they are good Christian women who know just how to deal with witches and keep their cool while others panic! The elder tree witch here is portrayed as cunning, untrustworthy, fearsome and greedy – shapeshifting and stealing milk from the farmer.

A man bought a farm in Somerset and moved in with his wife, his daughter and his elderly mother. His neighbours told him to be careful about the elders, but as there were no elder trees around the property he paid no heed. But one day, the farmer noticed that his cows were giving less and less milk. Someone else must be milking them! So he got up in the middle of the night to check on his cows.

As he walked across the pasture in the moonlight, he noticed the shadow of a tree by the hedge. A tree that had not been there the day before. This concerned the farmer, and in the morning he told the women of the house what he had seen. His wife looked alarmed. "Did you draw a cross in the mud in front of the gate?" she asked him. He shook his head.

The daughter went to the window and looked out. Her face turned pale and she ran around shutting the windows. "It's inside the gate! The tree! It's in the pasture with the cows! It's an elder!"

While all the yelling and running around was going on, old grandmother quietly got up, walked over to the fireplace and placed an iron shovel in the embers. Then she sat down, waiting.

The farmer gathered all his courage and loaded his gun with the silver buttons from his best coat and ran outside. He was frightened, but he was determined to save the cows, so he ran as close as he dared, aimed…and missed. His hands were shaking so badly he could not hold the gun steady, and the silver button flew past the tree. A terrible, screeching scream was heard, and the tree started moving towards him. The farmer yelled and turned on his heels and ran back to the house. His wife opened the door and shut it right behind him. Everyone, including the tree were screaming and hollering. In the midst of all the noise, old grandmother stood up. Calmly she went out of the back door and flung the shovelful of burning embers right into the branches of the elder tree. There was a terrible scream and the crackling of fire, and the elder tree went up in blue flame, until nothing was left of it but ashes. Granny picked up an ashen stick and drew the sign of the cross in the ashes.

The Edge of the Unknown

With the wildwood, like magic, there is always the edge of unknown, unknowable, unfamiliar and ever-changing. Folklore of the woods shows us through cultures and history how people saw the wild, how they connected nature to elements of the feminine, and what magic they considered to be held within the wildwood and its trees. Through story we have always explored what and how we 'know' the world. The fears and prejudices (as well as hopes and dreams) of everyday folks reveal themselves in these tales.

It is a wonderful image to think of witches working in their beautiful cottage gardens and gathering herbs and berries from hedgerows, walking through the woods and speaking to the trees – but many a wonderful (or regrettably accused) witch worked in the grit and gravel of cities and towns, bringing magic, healing and potions to crowded urban homes. Perhaps not working with herbs or trees at all. I absolutely acknowledge that many a witch has worked in the streets of busy market towns and within cramped terraced houses. Not every forest held a resident witch – but superstitions sure did like to suggest it. Trees, groves, springs, crossroads, waterfalls were places considered special and holding of a little something of old magic and as such were also connected to the witch in various ways. These were places of reverence and also of the unknown, where magic was always possible.

THE OLD WOMAN IN THE WOOD

A shortened version of the fairy tale that features in Volume 2 of Children's and Household Tales *by The Brothers Grimm (1815).*

The girl in this story feels keenly the dangers of being in the woods, she is an innocent in a place where witches and thieves lay in wait. But she also enjoys a bounty – the woods – and its animals provide everything she needs in way of food and shelter. She helps the caring dove (the white dove often symbolises The Holy Spirit, peace and hope) in return for the aid it offered her, she is doubly rewarded for her virtues of helpfulness and kindness with a wealthy husband after both their trials are ended.

In a vast forest, a servant-girl was travelling by coach with the wealthy family she served. They were travelling through deep dark forest when a band of robbers jumped out from behind the trees and set the horse loose and overturned the carriage! The robbers attacked the family, and all were killed save the servant girl, who leapt from the carriage and ran, hiding in the trees.

Soon she found herself lost and alone, she ran deeper and deeper into the woods to escape the horror of what she had seen and escaped. She grew so weary, and she despaired as she sat down by a tree to weep. But as she wept, a white dove appeared and gave her a small golden key, which he said to her would unlock a tree that held food within. Grateful, the servant girl used the key to open a little door in this enchanted tree, and within it lay a loaf of bread and cup of milk. The gifts continued... When darkness fell the dove gave her a key that provided, within other magical trees; a beautiful soft bed and in the morning another tree held splendid garments inlaid with gold and jewels. Life became peaceful for the girl in her newfound refuge – and she lived in this way there for some time. The trees held everything she needed, with the doves help.

One day, the dove asked for her help. "Of course," replied the girl, grateful for all the comfort the dove had given her. The dove told her to go to an old woman's house. He gave her the directions and told her to ignore the woman, but instead to walk straight into the little house and find a plain ring among many others and bring it back to him.

The girl followed the instructions. She went to the old woman's door and walked straight in, despite the old woman's cries of outrage. In the house lay hundreds of rings, laid over tables and tumbling down onto the floors. The servant-girl spied the plain ring inside a birdcage and returned to her refuge trees with it.

She waited and waited at the tree, but the dove didn't appear. She leant against a tree, concerned now. Suddenly the branches drew down, and twined around her: they were no longer branches, but arms. The tree was now a handsome man, who embraced her heartily, "You have saved me from the power of the old woman. She is a wicked witch. I am a prince and she changed me into a tree. For just two hours each day I could fly free as the white dove." The ring had allowed the prince to return to his human form, and all around they watched as his servants and all his horses, who had all also been changed into trees, were freed from the enchantment. The joyful royal party returned to the prince's kingdom, and he married the servant-girl, and in time she became a queen, and they both lived happily ever after.

REVEALING THE WYRD

I find the witch a wonderful guide in helping reveal the wyrd, wise and wonderful. The witch represents otherness: she is other than how women should be, how good Christian people *should* be, how civilised people should be: she is a rulebreaker, a gamechanger, agent of transformation and transgression. Otherness can be a waymarker of how we define ourselves and how others perceive us but in the wildwood, those waymarkers can get gobbled up by birds, or in the case of the previous story, we can be shapeshifted by a magic ring and we find ourselves lost or unrecognisable, reliant on the kindness of strangers.

The creatures we may meet in the dark forest help us make sense of our world and its boundary edges. When we enter the dark woods or in the witch's house, the laws of the civilised world and nature itself are suspended. Different rules are in play: we must follow their wyrd logic or suffer the consequences. Transformation is a common theme in folklore and fairytale – objects and people shift and change. This is why, in the woods and with the witch, it is not so clear to determine friend from foe, who we can trust from who we cannot. In these worlds we learn to listen to wise voices that come from many places and to follow our instincts.

VASILISSA THE BEAUTIFUL

Baba Yaga, in Slavic folklore lives deep in the heart of the woods, in the realm of the forest spirits and all the wild creatures. She lives in a little hut, often named Izbushka, that stands on stilt-like chicken legs and obeys her orders. In some tales, a fence surrounds the hut consisting of bones crowned with glowing skulls.

Baba Yaga is diversely depicted: sometimes she is an evil hag who eats children, and others she is a stern but kind elder, and wise woman. Many Baba Yaga stories may be understood as tales of initiation, sometimes but not always successful. To find Baba Yaga and seek her help, the hero(ine) would go into the deepest part of the forest, where they would come upon this little hut standing on chicken legs.

Like nature, Baba Yaga is unpredictable and should be approached with respect and reverence. The Baba Yaga story character represents the more wild and unpredictable force of nature, yet, she can also be generous. As a wise woman, she gives magical gifts and sound guidance for the future, though always with a test or a trial to go through in order to reach the desired goal.

This is a very short version of one of the most well-known tales featuring Baba Yaga. Beautiful Vasilissa finds a lot in her journey into the dark forest – fear, hope, revenge and the value of both rest and hard work – with the help of the tricksy Baba…(you can find the story of "Vasilissa the Beautiful" in many books of fairy tale, such as Russian Folk-tales, *translated from the Russian, by Leonard A. Magnus (1915) and* Russian Fairy Tales *by W. R. S. Ralston (1873).*

Even though young Vasilissa's stepmother and stepsisters treated her cruelly, she did her best to work hard and treasured the last gift from her mother, a very special little doll. But one evening, her stepsisters played a wicked trick to get rid of Vasilissa, letting all the candles in the house burn out. They ordered her out to find a flame from the old witch Baba Yaga. Baba Yaga lived in a hut in the forest, and it was said she ate up all who came her way. But Vasilissa, with her doll in her pocket, took courage and went on her way into the wild dark…

She journeyed for hours; she passed the horseman of white: Dawn. And then the horseman of red: Day. Through the forest shone rays of light. Vasilissa walked on all through the day, and finally, the horseman of black: Night passed her as she came to the clearing of Baba Yaga's hut. All around the hut stood a high fence made of human bones topped with skulls that blazed from within.

At this moment, from the forest, there arose a terrible noise. The branches of the trees crashed together, the leaves fell, and out of the trees came driving the Baba Yaga. In a mortar and pestle, she rode up to the hut where Vasilissa curtsied low and explained her plight. Baba scowled. "Now you are here, you must work. If you work well, maybe I will give you a light… Or maybe I will eat you. Who can tell? For now, serve up what's in the oven – tomorrow whilst I am away, you must clean, sweep and wash everything. And in the corn bin you will find two sorts of grain mixed up, wheat and oats. These you must separate into two heaps. You must also cook me a nice supper. If all is not done, I'll stick your bones onto my fence!"

That night when Baba was asleep, Vasilissa fed a little crumb to her doll and asked, "Little doll, what can I do?"

The doll answered, "Do not fear, Vasilissa. Rest now; the morning is wiser than the evening."

And when morning came, Baba Yaga rode out into the forest. And Vasilissa looked about her – and behold, every task was done! The dishes were washed, the floor was swept, and the wheat and the oats were separated into two heaps. Vasilissa took the doll from her pocket and gave it some breakfast. "My dear darling doll – you did this? You have saved me!"

The doll replied, "Now you have nothing to do but prepare Baba Yaga's supper." She climbed back into Vasilissa's pocket, "Keep heart, my little one."

On her return Baba inspected everything, "You have done well today – but how have you managed to do all the work I set you?"

"The blessing of my mother helped me," said Vasilissa.

"Agh!" choked Baba, "I can't be doing with blessed ones!" And she grabbed her broom and pushed Vasilissa out of the hut. Then she seized one of the lighted skulls from the fence and thrust it into Vasilissa's hand. "Here is the light for your step-mother's daughters. Take it and go, blessed one!"

So, with the skull to light her way and with the doll safe in her pocket, Vasilissa set off through the forest. But when she arrived home, the house was in darkness. The stepmother and her daughters had had no light all the time that Vasilissa had been away: every light they lit immediately went out. And now, the stepmother snatched the skull from Vasilissa, carried it into the parlour and set it on the table. "You've been long enough bringing it!" she said to Vasilissa.

"And what a hideous thing it is!" said the eldest stepsister.

"Couldn't you find anything better than that?" asked the second stepsister…

The skull glared at these ungrateful women with its burning eyes and jumped off the table. They were so frightened that they ran out of the room. The skull bounded after them as Vasilissa watched on. Stepmother and sisters ran from the house. The skull bounded after them. They ran into the forest. The skull bounded after them, its eyes burned brighter and brighter. It is said that the skull chased them all the way to the Baba Yaga's hut and that they were burnt to a crisp before Baba Yaga swallowed them up.

Both wildwood and witch have been destroyed in their droves over the centuries; perhaps both share a certain element of being under-valued and overlooked. It is always a good thing to speak, for many reasons, both of the trees and those that may have been lost in their shade. The symbol of the witch shows us something about the re-lationship between society and nature and how it is ever-changing. Our culture's disconnection from nature may have placed a shadow of fear and distrust over those connected to wild places.

Just as the trees connect the earth and the sky, the witch connects worlds as well – of folklore, fiction and real life, of gifts and ma-leficia, nurturing and destroying. Even today, the wildwood witch figure is powerful enough to cast a story of superstition into every woodland, every gnarled and crooked tree.

3

OTHER MAGICAL INHABITANTS OF THE WILDWOOD

The witch is not the only magical or fearsome creature to inhabit the dark woods. In the deep, dark forests, beautiful but dangerous spirits can be found, leading the unprepared astray. As far as I can tell, groups of supernatural and/or dangerous forest women appear in every country that has forests and woods (which is close to 90% of the planet's land mass, only the most extreme plains of sand and ice have no woods or forests at all). Journeying through different countries and cultures, you'll find many different witches and wild women of the woods. Narratives about – and a belief in – forest spirits were particularly strong in Sweden and Finland (where forests still cover vast areas in the Nordic countries: roughly 75% of Finland, almost 70% of Sweden). Lots of trees means lots of places to hide!

Female forest spirits are not only broader in number but, I think, more fascinating in their distinguishing features. From missing innards to lavish ornamentation and jewels, narratives vary widely from forest to forest, from an attractive young woman and fair folk to bad-tempered hags. Whilst some stories of witches could be connected to real life women who inhabited the dark woods, these next stories lie well beyond the realms and confines of civilisation: the rules of mankind hold no sway here. There are greater powers at play. These furious females are prone to acts of rage and revenge. It's time to meet just a few of these feral, mysterious, wild beings.

☾ The Wildalones – Samodiva (Bulgarian) and Water Nymphs – Rusalki (Slavic)

☾ Huldra and Skogsrå (Scandinavian)

☾ Wood Wives (German and European)

☾ The Witch Maidens (Slavic)

☾ Muma Padurii (Romanian)

☾ The Green Ladies (British)

☾ Green Men and Wild Men (British and Germanic)

☽ Bogles (British and Scottish)

☽ The Marsh Witches (Danish)

☽ The Night Owls – Strix (Greco-Roman)

THE WILDALONES

Samodiva (Bulgarian) and Water nymphs – Rusalki (Slavic)

Once upon a time, wild maidens of otherworldly beauty lived deep within the forest. Their skin was as pale as silver birch, eyes as sparkling as morning dew, and their hair golden as the sun. And quietly, softly, away from mortal eyes, the samodivi came out only in the night, bathing under ancient oak trees, dancing below moonlight – until the rooster's cry sends them hiding from the dawn, back inside a cave that neither man nor beast could enter...

The samodiva, are wild, woodland beings of Bulgarian folklore described as nymphs, witches and/or demons. Their name in common translation is the enchanting *wildalone* – from *samo* (alone) and *diva* (wild). They can be found in the woodlands and by water sources from spring until autumn and they may be seen dancing in forest glades at night. They are a joyful symbol of the coming spring, the awakening of nature, but woe betide the traveller who happens upon the samodivi (plural of samodiva) and beholds their dance under the full moon. In some tales, they drag shepherds who happen upon them over treetops before tearing them to pieces. Stories describe them as wild beings but also divine; in some legends samodivi are the daughters of the Thracian mother goddess figure Bendis.*

In similar Slavic folklore, the rusalka/rusalki are considered wild

---

* Thrace is an area closely connected to ancient Greece, encapsulating areas of Greece, Bulgaria and Turkey. Bendis had many forms in this culture including huntress and goddess of wilderness.

water beings – lurking in lakes, rivers and swamplands, but they could also climb trees and join other rusalki to dance in meadows and woodlands. A feature of the stories of both samodiva and rusalka is that they only dance in certain periods of the year, usually the spring and summer. *Rusalki* were believed to be at their most dangerous during the 'Rusalka week' in early June when they leave their watery homes at night to swing on the branches of birch and willow trees. Swimming during this week was ill-advised – lest they leap from their branches to drag you down to the riverbed.

In Polish versions of the rusalka story, she is a being that is not born but made. A woman becomes a rusalka after drowning, committing suicide or being murdered by male relatives or lovers near water, suggesting her actions may be in revenge (so often the way – from ancient tales to modern newspaper headlines – often women described as violent, hostile, mad or wild, are acting in self-defence, seeking escape or retribution).

TREE-TALES: WILLOW

In Slavic folklore willows are trees of magic, witches and the devil: the rusalki we just met, lived in willow trees.

Most willow species thrive close to water or in damp places and so a lot of willow folklore has a watery theme. The moon also recurs as an association, the movement of water being affected by the moon. The cascading, drooping shape of the weeping willow *(Salix babylonica)* makes it a symbol of sorrow and grief.

Witch's Garden: Plants in Folklore, Magic and Traditional Medicine by Sandra Lawrence names willow as traditionally a wood of the gallows (and we're back to sorrow again), but a willow wand repelled evil or made a useful water-divination rod. Its healing properties made willow a sought-after tree by the village wise-woman, and the willow's healing and superstition became one and the tree became called 'witch's tree' (as many trees were, as of course, many had healing qualities that afforded them similar connections, or particular warding qualities, like the rowan tree).

THE HULDRA

(Norway and Scandinavia) and Skogsrå (Sweden)

The huldra – half-woman, half-tree – lives in the deep forests of Scandinavian lore. She is beautiful from the front, but her back reveals gnarled tree roots and rotting wood: an indicator of her true nature, perhaps, or her wildness within, part of her will always belong to the woods. Her beautiful face is appealing, and she is known to lure men away to do their bidding with their beautiful songs. The huldra may be seen as sly and sensual, appearing to seduce humans, spiriting them away to their dwellings, or occasionally stealing and exchanging babies with their own (much like fairies were wont to do with changelings in the British Isles). However, most Norse folklore describes the huldra as keepers or wardens, symbolic of the dangers of the wild forests and mountains. In some tales, they herd cattle through the forest, and they might be heard calling and singing through the gloom of an evening wood. Huldra might also be associated with female magic workers or oracles, who practised *seiðr* magic*, telling and shaping the future.

"She is a witch who takes the form of a lovely woman, and meeting humans in the woods she lures them to follow her. Her dwelling is in the mountains, which she opens with a magic word. Inside is a gorgeous palace, filled with immense riches, and having dining-rooms containing splendidly decorated tables laden with

---

* Seiðr is a form of magic, meaning cord or string in old norse, *Seiðr* is connected to both the seeing and the weaving of the future.

all the food a Norwegian enjoys most, served on golden dishes. He
who eats of these things is thenceforth in the power of the huldra.
Occasionally he wins free; but never afterwards is he as he was.

In the country the folks speak of idiots and
madmen as being 'mountain-taken', believing
that these are victims of the huldra's wiles.

If, however, the involuntary guest refuses to partake of the
magic dishes in the mountain passes, he sees before his eyes
the dishes of exquisite food turning to pinecones and slabs of
earth, while the huldra loses her fascination, and can no longer
hide from him the cow's tail by which she is to be known,
nor can she keep him prisoner any longer. Without knowing
how, he finds himself back in the woods on the mountainside;
and he cannot discover the entrance to the fairy palace."

Beatrix Jungman, Norway (1905)

Throughout the northern lands, the name of this forest spirit changes, with regional additions, such as a tail, hooves and furry legs, indicative of her liminality and wildness. She partly belongs to the wildwood and its beasts and holds the forest realm's power (and deception abilities). As a plural, the word *huldrefolk*, meaning 'hidden', can be used for all manner of supernatural beings. Huldra, in the singular, signifies this specific female forest spirit (and her hidden side).

She may also be known as skogsrå – forest keeper, forest maiden or forest hag – in Sweden. She has the same hollow tree back as the huldra. She seduces men and keeps something of them as their soul stays behind with her. Another similar Swedish folkloric figure is Grankotte-Maja (Spruce Cone Maja) or Talle-Maja (Pine-tree Maja).* She, too, lures men into the forest with her beauty and distorts their vision.

---

* Maja is a girl's name that might be likened to Mary in English-speaking countries.

WOOD-WIVES AND WITCH MAIDENS

In Germanic folklore, the wood-wives are sometimes described as fairy folk – beautiful tiny beings with pale skin and long flowing gowns who dwell deep in the heart of the ancient forests. In other stories, they bear closer semblance to the haunting skogsrå or witch-like figures. Also called wish-wives, moss-maidens and wood-women.

> *"We have seen that the wish-wives appear on pools and lakes in the depth of the forest: it is because they are likewise wood-wives, and under this character they suggest further reflections. The old sacred forest seems their favourite abode: as the gods sat enthroned in the groves, on the trees, the wise women of their train and escort would seek the same haunts."*

Jacob Grimm, *Deutsche Mythologie* (1835)

Like the dryads of ancient Greek myths, their lives were intertwined with the health of the trees. If the trunk of a tree was broken or its bark ripped off, a wood-wife may die. Wood-wives might be lured to homes around edges of the forest by smells of baking, and may even approach and request cakes, or sneak a meal from bubbling cooking pots. In old Germanic customs one might, when baking, make a little extra loaf to be left out in the woods for the wood-wives. In thanks she might teach humans herb-craft and healing, help with household tasks or leave wood chips that would turn into gold coins, on the condition that their source was kept secret.[4]

> *"According to certain tales of the peasantry, a demonic creature dwells near Leutenberg and on the left bank of river Saale, called the Buschgroßmutter ('Shrub Grandmother'). She has many daughters, called Moosfräuleins ('Moss Ladies'), with whom she roves around the country at certain times and upon certain holy nights. It is not good to meet her, for she has wild, staring eyes and*

crazy, unkempt hair. Often, she drives around in a little cart or
wagon, and at such times it is wise to stay out of her way… She is
essentially the same spirit as Hulda or Bertha, the Wild Huntress
– to whom local tales ascribe a following of children under the
guise of the Heimchen (dwarfs, pixies, brownies, hobgoblins)
who constitute her attendants in the area she frequents. […]

Sometimes, however, the moss-women and their relatives the
wood-maidens are more friendly to man and will help him
industriously in the harvest-field; they have even been known to
enter his service and bring prosperity to all his undertakings."

Mrs J. H. Philpot, *The Sacred Tree* (1897)

THE WOOD MAIDEN AND THE GOLDEN BIRCH LEAVES

I found many versions of this story, including Favourite Fairy
Tales Told in Czechoslovakia *by Virginia Haviland (1966) and*
Sixty Folk-Tales from Exclusively Slavonic Sources, *translated*
by Albert Henry Wratislaw (1889).

The name Betushka is surely derived from the Latin for birch
tree, Betula. *And here the trees and wood maiden captivate this*
little girl who clearly has a love and connection to the birch
forest. Betushka finds that the great riches within this place
come in many forms: food for her goats and a place where she
can spin, and within the trees she also finds music, magic and
golden gifts from the wood maiden.

Once upon a time, there was a girl named Betushka. She lived
with her mother in the tumbledown cottage and two goats.
They were poor, but they had a happy life.

Every day from spring until autumn Betushka drove the goats
to graze in the beautiful birch woods. Her mother would pack

some bread and an empty spindle into her bag. Betushka would spin flaxen thread while she watched the goats. Betushka sang and danced along her path through the birch wood, and when the goats grazed, she would sit down under a tree. There she twirled her spindle and flax and sang merrily, whilst the goats nibbled on grass amongst the trees.

One fine spring day, when Betushka was dancing and singing on her path, suddenly a most beautiful maiden appeared before her. She wore a floating gown of forest green and a wreath of wild blossoms crowned her golden hair.

In a sweet voice, she asked, "Betushka, do you like to dance?

At this, Betushka exclaimed, "Oh! I could dance all day long!"

"Come then, let us dance together."

The maiden called upon the birds sitting in the birch trees to sing their music; nightingales, larks, gold finches, thrushes, and mockingbirds sang sweet melodies. Betushka's heart filled with joy. The maiden danced so beautifully that Betushka couldn't take her eyes from her. She forgot her goats; she forgot her spinning. On and on, they danced till evening when the sun began to set. The music ceased, and Betushka now saw her spindle, barely half-filled with thread and she burst into tears, reproaching herself for forgetting her work.

The maiden laughed, "Worry not, dear one," she said, twining the flax around a slender birch tree. The spindle hummed and grew thick with thread. By the time the sun had dropped from sight, the maiden disappeared, and all the flax was spun. Betushka journeyed home and gave her mother the full spindle.

The next day Betushka arrived singing in the birch wood. The beautiful maiden appeared at noon and smiled at Betushka as she put her arm about her, they whirled round and round.

Again, Betushka forgot her tasks; again, she saw nothing but the maiden, and heard nothing but the enchanting birdsong.

As the sun was setting, the maiden handed Betushka her bag; she had filled it with something light and told her not to look into it before reaching home, and with these words, she disappeared into the setting sunlight.

Betushka started home but could not resist peeking into the bag; it was full of dry birch leaves! She wept angrily and tossed some of the leaves out of the bag but stopped; she could not be wasteful – they would make good bedding for the goats.

On arriving home, Betushka confessed the whole story to her mother about the maiden. "That is the wood lady!" said her mother. "Wood maidens dance at midday and midnight; you might not have escaped alive, but the wood maidens give rich presents to those who find their favour."

Betushka remembered her bag. She opened it once more and gasped! The birch leaves had turned to gold! Plenty for a fine new home and dairy cows and pretty dresses for the rest of their days. Nothing, however, gave Betushka quite so much delight as dancing with the beautiful maiden. Often, she sang in the birch woods but never again did her beloved wood maiden appear.

TREE TALES: BIRCH (BETULA)

Bundles of birch have long been used to drive out malevolence in its many forms. Magically minded folks might use a besom broom made of birch to cleanse and purify their homestead – most broomsticks were once commonly made of birch twigs. Birch kindling was used to light fires to welcome the first sunrise of spring or summer, and birch wood was burned to aid concentration and lift the spirits.

Within the branches of birch trees, there may be found dense, nest-like clusters of twigs. These are the work of a fungus which prompts this growth and then feeds on the new shoots. These growths are known widely in England and Scotland as witches' brooms or witches' knots, and it was thought that they appeared after witches had flown over the tree; the more clusters, the more witches had been by.

In Celtic mythology, the silver birch *(Betula pendula)* is a tree of beginnings and came to symbolise renewal and purification. It was celebrated during the festival of Samhain. Samhain was considered the start of the Celtic year, when purification was important, and people used bundles of birch twigs to drive out the spirits of the old year.

THE THREE WITCH MAIDENS

In Slavic mythology jezinka are a wood nymph or demon, they may appear as beautiful and finely dressed young witch maidens. But they also enjoy putting people to sleep and gouging out their eyes and stealing children to feast upon. Ruth Manning-Sanders wrote several fairy tales featuring the witch maidens – an anglicised term for these jezinkas who gather in sisterhoods. This one is "The Three Witch Maidens" drawn from her book of the same name, published in 1977.

A shepherd boy was watching over his sheep in a meadow, when he saw a very tall and beautiful tree. Inspired to climb up it, he ascends for a long time before emerging onto a land of copper; there is a copper palace, surrounded by a copper forest, and a spring of copper flowing like water and tinkling gently. Above the spring a copper bird is perched asleep on the low branches of a copper tree. It is the only living thing in sight. The land around is silent as death.

He looks at the tree where the bird is sleeping and decides to climb this one too. And after more climbing he arrives in a land of silver: a silver palace, a silver forest, and a silver bird perched above a silver spring in a very tall silver tree. The shepherd once more launches himself up that tree, and emerges into a kingdom of shining gold, including a golden bird in a golden tree. But this tree is polished smooth; the shepherd has no hope of climbing it, so, he turns around and climbs all the way down, down the silver tree, down the copper tree, down the tall tree to the meadow. Exhausted; he settles at the foot of the tree and falls asleep.

When he awakes, he is not alone. A small green frog is trying to climb the tall tree, despite being unable to reach the lowest branch, the frog exclaims to the shepherd, "I am a queen who ruled over those three kingdoms! But the witch maidens turned me into this shape and stole my kingdoms from me. They have taken the form of birds, only taking human form at dawn, when each one discards her feathers and bathes in their springs. I wish to steal these feathers and demand the witch maidens return my kingdoms, but I can't climb this tree."

The shepherd, moved by her story, offers to act on her behalf and take the feathers. So when, once again he climbs the tree and he reaches the copper kingdom, he hides and waits for dawn. The bird flies down to the copper waters, shrugs off her feathers and goes to bathe in the spring as a woman. The shepherd snatches her feathers and bolts up the copper tree into the silver kingdom, where he steals the feathers of the witch maiden in this realm, and once more again in the gold kingdom, then throws himself down again as fast as he can and tumbles out into the meadow with the witches hot on his heels.

"Give us back our feathers!" the witch maidens howl, for their magic powers are connected to their feathers and they cannot curse him. The frog queen demands that her kingdoms be returned. The witch maidens have little choice, so holding hands, they circle the tree and sing.

The incantation brings the copper kingdom down, then the silver, and finally the gold, stretching across the landscape in a vast sprawl. What's more, the kingdoms are suddenly filled with people, joyfully flinging open doors and windows. The frog is transformed, and she is once again a beautiful, powerful queen. The shepherd returns the feathers to their owners, and as birds of copper, silver and gold – the witch maidens fly away. The queen, in gratitude, marries the shepherd amidst the celebrations of three kingdoms.

Vengeful Spirits

Forests and woods around the world hold stories of the protective feminine spirits or deities that watch over them – and the fates that may befall disrespectful visitors. These beings may inhabit the heart of the wilderness, guarding its secrets and guiding those who enter their realm. They may be nurturing figures, but they can also be brutal, violent killers, merciless in their ferocity if the sanctity of their wilderness is under threat. Their presence in myths and legends highlights the deep reverence that ancient cultures held for the power and mystery of the forested landscapes and may remind us of humanity's responsibility to respect and preserve the natural world and all within it.

Muma Padurii

The Romanian "mother of the forest" may be depicted as an old crone who lives in a hut/cabin or an old tree deep in the darkest corners of the woods. She cares for plants and animals in the forest, brewing potions, nursing injured animals and healing dying trees. Sometimes she is depicted as a mischievous magical crone, taking the form of wild animals; in others, she is a woman who looks like a tree, with dry, cracked skin like bark, clothing of moss and long tangled hair that falls in vine-like strands.

But often she represents something grander: an embodiment of the forest, ruler of everything that is born, grows and lives within it. She also keeps unwanted trespassers away by driving them mad or scaring them with her frightful appearance, harming those who injure the forest, like loggers who disregard the rules of the forest and those who pick berries on certain days of the year when wild animals would be in greater need. Sometimes she sets upon those foolish enough to walk alone at night without due respect to the forest. And, fair warning, she has been known to eat the bodies of those she kills.[5]

Green Ladies

'Green Ladies' can be found as folkloric figures throughout the British Isles. They often represent an otherworldly spirit of the wild natural world and are protective of it – as benevolent guardians of nature or a fiercer presence. For some, the colour green, as you might guess, symbolises a connection to nature but also a certain unruliness: fairies were often said to dress in green and Robin Hood is enduringly green clad. In some Scottish folktales the *Baobhan Sith* wear long green dresses that conceal the hooves she has instead of feet (we will meet the *Baobhan Sith* very shortly). Green clothing also allows such beings to blend into the forestscape, to watch (and judge) unseen.

As legendary folklorist Katharine Mary Briggs describes them, "the Green Ladies of Scotland were connected with the dead, and so naturally wore green, for green is the Celtic colour of death."[6] In other stories, Green Ladies are closer to ghosts, fairy folk or to the figure of the Greek dryad, nymph or nature spirit who dwells within specific trees. And in some cases the Green Ladies are the very trees themselves...

THE GREEN LADIES OF THE HILL

Found in Forgotten Folktales of the English Counties *by Ruth L. Tongue (1970).*

This tale tells of greed and its repercussions, here, justice is served by the Green Ladies to the brothers not living in right relationship to the land. The brother's folly is their inability to listen to their ancestors, respect the land or being grateful for what they had. The youngest brother ultimately profits for following these virtues.

Once there stood three tall trees on a hill. On moonlit nights, singing could be heard, and three Green Ladies danced under the stars. Every year on Midsummer's Eve, the farmer of that land climbed the hill to lay a posy of primroses at the roots of each tree.* The leaves rustled, the sun shone out, and his farm prospered. The farmer said to his three sons, "Our luck lies up there. When I'm dead, don't forget to do as I did, and my father did before me."

When the old man died, the big farm was divided; the eldest brother took a huge slice, and the next brother took another, and that left the youngest with a strip of poor, rough ground

* In the UK primrose don't flower in June, this may be a suggestion that the farmer has to find a rare and magical plant to offer these special ladies. Or that all is not quite as it seems, as is often the way of folk tales, little clues in the story tell us this is a tale that is only a half-truth.

at the foot of the hill, but he set to work and sang as he worked.

One day his brothers came to see him. Their big farms were not doing well, and when they saw his rich little barley fields and loaded fruit trees, and his herbs growing so green and smelling so sweet, they were angry and jealous. The youngest brother told them "I have only done as Father told us and to-night it is Midsummer's Eve – so we must lay primrose posies for the trees."

But the older brothers did not listen, deaf with greed. "The hill is mine," cried the eldest. "Don't let me see you up there again. As for the trees, I need timber for my new barn, so I'll be cutting one down."

The next day was Midsummer's Day, and the eldest brother came with carts and men and axes.

When he laid his axe to the first tree, it screamed, but he went on hacking. The wind howled, and the two other trees lashed their branches in anger. And as the tree toppled it was on top of the eldest brother, crushing his bones and killing him instantly. Now there were only two Green Ladies left to dance on moonlit nights.

Soon the jealous second brother came to the hill, "This is my hill now, I'll build a fence round my hill, and I'll cut down one of the trees to make it with!" That night, there was no dancing, there was no music, but the crying of many leaves. The next morning the second brother came with an axe, and the two trees shuddered. Once again screaming was heard as the second tree fell, the last tree lifted a great branch and brought it down on the second brother's head, cleaving his skull in two.

The youngest brother now had all three farms, but he still lived near the hill and the lonely Green Lady. And sometimes she would dance alone to a sad tune on moonlit nights, and he left bunches of primroses at her roots. Many won't climb One Tree Hill, for it holds sadness and danger; it now belongs to the last and lonely Green Lady, and she still rages at the greed of men.

THE GREEN MAN AND WILD MEN

Not all spirits of the forest were female. Peering from the ceilings of cathedrals and the gables of churches throughout England (and far beyond) there can be found a pre-Christian symbol and face of nature. A face surrounded by leaves, often oak in English examples, though other vegetation such as vines, branches and ivy can be seen as well. A reminder of the Old Ways hidden in plain sight.

"Green man" was a term in common use at least since the 1600s from accounts of festivals and pageants (it was and continues to also be a hugely popular name for English pubs).

*"Two disguised, called Greene-men, their habit Embroydred and Stitch'd on with Ivie leaves with blacke-side, having hanging to their shoulders, a huge black shaggie Hayre, Savage-like, with Ivie Garlands upon their heads..."**

In her 1936 novel, *The Goat Foot God,* Dion Fortune, British occultist and author, connected the Green Man to Pan and wood spirits: *"I suppose you know who the Green Man is? He's Pan... He's Jack-In-The-Green, the wood-spirit."*

A few years later, in 1939, Julia Somerset (often known by her title,

---

* From a 1610 publication; *Chester's triumph in honor of her prince As it was performed upon S. Georges Day 1610 in the foresaid citie.* These foliage clad figures have held various names in English folk festivals and processions including Jack in the Green/Jack o' the green – who are still involved in seasonal festivities, particularly around May Day – to herald in the Summer.

Lady Raglan), wrote an article for the Folklore Society Journal in which she applied the name "Green Man" to both the design of the foliate head and a character from traditional folk culture. Lady Raglan grouped these figures together and collectively called them "the Green Man" as a remnant of ancient pre-Christian folklore. Most recent research by women such as botanist Kathleen Basford, photographer Ruth Wylie, and historian Marcia MacDermott has created a wealth of research on the cultural significance and origins of the figure around the world. Basford refers to it as the "spiritual dimension of nature" in architecture, showing 'Green Men' from England, such as at Ely Cathedral, c.1335, all the way back to foliate heads found in artefacts from ancient Mesopotamia and Istanbul dating back to the earliest centuries BCE.

To some the Green Man is a nature spirit of ancient woodlands; a symbol fruitfulness and spirit of the great forests that once covered the land; a symbol of a time and wilderness lost, lurking in the vaulted corners of church ceilings. To others he is a form of the Wild Man or even a deity. While the Green Man is an image and idea whose complete meaning has been lost through time, it is hard to imagine that he is not in some ways deeply linked with our ancient woodlands.

> *"Two millennia old or older, the Green Man is the vibrant spirit of the wild wood, of vegetation in leaf or bud, of spring, pool and river, earth and sky, indeed the totality of Nature. His voice is the hiss of high wind in ash and oak. And his profundity those sudden silences of a forest when all Nature seems to hold her breath. When we hear or feel him no more mankind will have run its course."*

Ronald Millar, *The Green Man* (1997)

The Wild Men or *woodwose* were particularly popular mythical figures from the legend and folklore of medieval Europe; they appear in the art and literature, representing uncultivated wilderness and primal nature, often bedecked in lots of wild hair and crowns or garments of leaves.

The folkloric motif of the 'wild man in the woods' is both ancient and largely universal; we can see it appearing in stories ranging from Enkidu in the Babylonian Epic of Gilgamesh to early Arthurian legends of Merlin and the Green Knight. And around Europe in the Middle Ages, wild men (and women) were more than just characters in stories: there existed outcasts who, due to various reasons (trauma, poverty, 'madness'), and some by choice (like religion or social outcasts) – withdrew from society and lived in the wildernesses. Like the Green Man, images of wild men appear in many churches and cathedrals in the UK (Canterbury Cathedral is an example). The image of the wild man also appears on coats-of-arms, especially in Germany, well into the sixteenth century, as a symbol of strength.

One might consider more modern legends of bigfoot, yetis, and abominable snowmen as drawn from older wild man myths. Popular fictional characters such as Tarzan and Mowgli are modern renderings of the wild man archetype – both characters represent primal aspects of humanity, raised by animals in the jungle, they exemplify the idea of humans reverting to a more instinctual and feral state. Tarzan embodies strength and agility as he navigates the African wilderness, while Mowgli, in Kipling's *Jungle Book,* straddles the worlds of animals and humans, navigating the duality of human nature. These characters tap into the enduring fascination with the wild, speaking to the tensions between civilisation and the call of the wild within us all. Interestingly, both Tarzan and Mowgli are ultimately drawn back into civilisation by women, Jane and Messua, respectively. In contrast to 'wild women' we have met such as the samodivi and huldra who lure men from cities into the woods.

> *"The medieval Wild Man was a godless and repulsive*
> *savage like the distant barbarians of classical geographers.*
> *But he lurked in the woods of Europe like the satyrs. His*
> *function in the medieval imagination was to be a bogey in*

a world obsessed with religious and social order, an awful warning of the consequences of a lack of either…"

Ronald Hutton, *The Pagan Religions of the Ancient British Isles: their nature and legacy* (1991)

BOGLES

"It happened at that time that the bog was frequented by a huge bogle or ghost, who was of a most mischievous disposition, and took particular pleasure in abusing every traveller who had occasion to pass through the place betwixt the twilight at night and cock-crowing in the morning."

Folk-lore and legends Scotland (1889)

Tales of bogles, bogies, hobgoblins, bogeys and boggarts can be found through the British Isles. They are "names given to a whole class of mischievous, frightening and even dangerous spirits whose delight it is to torment mankind".[7] Bogles seem more popular in tales from northern England and Scotland. They are often found playing pranks and causing trouble. Bogles inhabit dark, secluded places, such as forests, bogs and marshes, caves or abandoned buildings. Folk traditions suggest protections from Bogles common to many other fairy folk – like appeasing offerings of milk or honey, wearing protective charms or objects made of iron.

JEANIE THE FURIOUS BOGLE

You can find a version of this tale of Jeanie in A Month in Yorkshire *by Walter White (1861), who describes Jeanie as from the species of "the boggle-boggarts – a Yorkshire fairy tribe", as well as more recently in* The Book of English Folk Tales *by Sybil Marshal, (1981). Many variations of the story exist of an angry Jeanie; she is described in varying stories as a fairy, bogle or woodland sprite. I rather like her as a bogle. I also thought this tale was a useful reminder just how infuriating it is to have one's peace disturbed, and it's never warranted to holler at women (it tends to make us justifiably angry...)*

Mulgrave Wood in Yorkshire (UK) was once, they say, the woodland home to bogles. Unlike the hobgoblin and house spirits that may help humans occasionally, the wise woman knows the bogles should be left well alone. The chief bogle was called Jeanie, known to be fierce even as bogles go.

But one day, a farmer wished to make the acquaintance of Jeanie. Perhaps he did not really believe in her and wanted to meet her for himself. Or perhaps, being brave on beer one night, he took a wager. Either way, he saddled his horse and set out to seek Jeanie in the woods. Once into Mulgrave Wood, he sought out her dwelling, a cave on a rocky slope. Leaning from his saddle, he called her loudly by name. "Jeanie!" he hollered, "Jeanie! Are you there? Come out, lass. I want a word wi' thee!"

Jeanie, whose peaceful day had been disturbed, answered his call. With her lips snarling, she came out of her cave like a whirlwind, brandishing in her hand her magic wand. The farmer's horse was terrified and bolted at a frenzied gallop through the trees as though all the devils in hell were behind it. The farmer now understood that his attentions towards her were not welcome. Jeanie was fast and kept pace with the horse, but before them lay a stream, so the farmer set his horse to jump. As the horse rose onto its back legs to leap, Jeanie's wand descended. The horse made it to the homeward side of the water. The farmer did not – for Jeanie's wand had sliced him clean in two. And never again did a farmer or anyone else, bother that particular lady of the woods.

THE BLOODSUCKING BAOBHAN SITH

The Baobhan Sith *(pronounced Baa-van Shee) is a spirit found in the mountains and forests of the Highlands of Scotland. Not to be trifled with, the Baobhan Sith drinks the blood of young men who tramp the highlands and the night wilds. Fiercely protective of deer of her wild domain. She may take forms of wild animals – raven, crow or wolf – or as a beautiful maid in a green dress, with cloven hooves hidden under her long gown. Some see the Baobhan Sith as type of a vampire and omen of death. This is a short version of the often-told tale, a warning to all who stalk the wilds…*

You can find tales of the Baobhan Sith in such books as Scottish Folk-Lore and Folk Life *by Donald Mackenzie (1935),* An Encyclopedia of Fairies Hobgoblins, Brownies, Bogies, And Other Supernatural Beings *by Katharine Briggs (1978) and* Myths, Gods & Fantasy *by Pamela Allardice (1991).*

Four men had been hunting through the Scottish Highlands, and after a long day they are delighted to find a bothy.* They tie up their horses and head inside pleased to see a hearth

---

* A little hut or cottage, used for shelter in the Highlands.

stacked with wood ready to light a fire and four chairs waiting for them. They settle in, share a wee dram of whisky, and enjoy the warm fire as night falls around them.

In high spirits they declare that the only thing that would make the night more pleasant would be four maidens to join them. Not a moment after they say this, four beautiful maidens tap at the door and ask to be let in, saying they had become lost in the wilderness. They dance and sing, entrancing the men. But one of the men longs for his dear wife and is more reticent, he pauses just long enough to hear the scuffing of hooves and see a drop of blood splash upon the floor, he knows now what these creatures are, and he bolts for the door. Seeking refuge among the horses and their iron shod hooves, the fourth Baobhan Sith watches the last man all night but cannot get close – while her three sisters are having a jolly time inside the bothy. When daylight breaks, all four maidens are gone, back to the wilds. Finally able to return to the bothy, the last man finds his three companions with their necks and bellies cut open by sharp nails and their innards devoured by the ferocious teeth of the Baobhan Sith.

Marsh Witches

Some forests have boggy parts, others border marshland and in these wild in-between places there is much magic to be found...so I'm sneaking it in here!

"Down in the water between strange, fine plants, strange animals move, silently they slide out and into the glass-green, mysterious forests [...] when the sun goes to rest, when the marsh woman in the bright summer night brews her bubbling

*drink that smells of mint and honeysuckle, and the white
flower splendor of the* skarntyde* *shines through the fog,
when glow worm with his lantern searches for his beloved
in the wild forest of grass and flowers, while the nightingale
sings, then the meadow bares its soul, showing itself in all its
bewitching splendor to the one who dares to enter the mist."*

**Vand-og stenhoejsplanter en vejledning for havevenner
(Water and Stone Plants: a garden guide)† (1917)**

When the fog lays heavy over the valleys, moors and marshland
the Danish might say *Mosekonen brygger* which translates as "the
marsh woman is brewing". *Mosekonen* is a woman or witch (sometimes depicted as a normal looking woman, or sometimes as more
troll-like or witchy in appearance) who lives hidden in the marshes
and moorland. She is known for brewing in big kettles or cauldrons,
and you will know when she is brewing, because that is when there
is fog and mist over the marshes and moors.

In northern England and Scotland, the marsh witch and moss-maid-
en equivalent may perhaps be such ill-reputed river-demons as the
Shellycoat, whose clattering coat of shells serves to warn his victims
that he means to lure them to the river and drown them. Whereas,
around the Midlands and Northern England there is Jenny Greenteeth
and unnamed female river hags whose long green hair resembles the
water weed that drags their prey down toward sharp teeth and claws.

*   "Skarntyde" is Norwegian for "poison hemlock" (*Conium maculatum*)

†   This is from the section on aquatic and moss plants by Jens K. Jørgensen
and might just be the most poetic garden book I've ever found and a wonderful
reminder that folklore can permeate everyday life and many a book.

THE MARSH WOMAN'S WARNING

Danish fairy tale author Hans Christian Anderson mentions the marsh or moor woman in several of his fairy tales and describes her brewery, within mounds of earth amongst the marshes, as full of toads and snakes. This fairy tale from Anderson, features the Marsh Woman and another famed marsh resident: the will-o'-the-wisp. First recorded in 1661, Will-o'-the-Wisp is derived from Will, short for William, and wisp is a bunch of hay used as a torch. Very much like Jack o' lantern for Halloween pumpkins being a shortened version of Jack of the Lantern. Other names for the phenomenon are spunkie, walking fire, elf-fire, fox fire, fools fire, and corpse light. The phosphorescent phenomenon is a flickering light that appears in marshy or boggy areas at night. The scientific explanation is that natural gases, like methane, ignite and create a ghostly glow. This has led to myths and legends about mischievous or malevolent spirits that lure travellers astray.

This is a version of "The Will-o'-the-Wisps are in town, says the Marsh Woman" a translation of Hans Christian Andersen's "lygtemændene ere i byen, sagde mosekonen" first published in 1865. Anderson's tale of the Marsh Woman's warning is a beautiful one of memory and story, and that great stories may be held in the liminal places of marshland and magic. It is also a reminder to respect the natural world; an environmental warning through supernatural means. England too has lost much of its marshland, so this could be a warning for many countries — destroy the marshland and the Will o' the Wisps will come walking!

There was a man who once knew many stories, but they had slipped away from him. He remembered so well all the various forms in which Story had come to him, as a beautiful maiden, with a wreath of thyme in her hair, and a beechen branch in her hand, and with eyes that gleamed like deep woodland lakes in the sunshine. Sometimes Story appeared in the guise of a pedlar, with boxes of silver ribbon fluttering with verses and inscriptions. At other times she appeared as a grandmother with silvery hair, who knows so well how to tell about the oldest times, long before the princesses spun with the golden spindles. The man longed to find Story once more and realised, "I must go forth and seek out in the country, out in the woods!"

He journeyed past where the nightingale sings among the beech-leaves. Where, in the dark days of winter, the trees told of the Wild Chase on stormy nights. Down he went, through the great avenue of wild chestnut trees, through the alder grove, over the hill covered with red-thorn and broom. And then, as the sun went down, he found himself overlooking marsh and moorland covered with low mist. The Marsh Woman was at her brewing. As dusk fell and the moon shone bright, a woman appeared before him and said, "I am the Marsh Woman who brews. I belong to the witch folk."

The man asked her about Story, "By my cauldron!" exclaimed the woman, "Story, she's the oldest of us all, I know her well. I have often gone into the forest and met the Story-maiden".

"You know all about Story!" said the man, delighted.

Answered the Marsh Woman, "Stories and poetry? Yes, and one can brew all their chatter, I have a whole cupboard-full of words in bottles!" And she showed him, in the midst of the misty moor, a cupboard hewn from a great stump of alder. The Marsh Woman said that this was open to everyone in the land, if they only knew where the cupboard stood.

But then the Marsh Woman warned him, "I have a true story that you must heed. You must beware of the Will-o'-the-Wisps. There was a great commotion yesterday out here in the marsh, a christening feast! Twelve little Will-o'-the-Wisps were born. I sat there on the cupboard and had all the twelve little new-born Will-o'-the-Wisps upon my lap. Now, Will-o'-the-Wisps – they may run about in the country and through the world. They can float into the heart and mind of man and speak and move for him. The Will-o'-the-Wisp may take whatever form he likes and can act in their spirit.

"But that's not all! For if, in the course of the year, the Wisp can lead three hundred and sixty-five people astray, then they attain the great honour of being a runner before the devil's stage coach. Then they'll wear clothes of fiery yellow and breathe forth flames. All Will-o'-the-Wisps aspire to play so distinguished a part. If they fail, they must come back into the marsh and will be imprisoned in a dead tree; and that's the most terrible punishment that can be inflicted on a lively Will-o'-the-Wisp.

"Now, all this I told to the twelve little Wisps whom I had on my lap, and who seemed quite crazy with joy. The little flames all fancied themselves clad in fiery yellow clothes, breathing flames.

"'The mortals are drying up our marshes,' cried the new-born Wisps. 'They've taken to draining them all. What will our descendants do? We must blaze brighter!' And with this the dogs and witches of the Wild Chase went rushing over the land, towards the town – carrying the Will-o'-the-Wisps with them!

"I'll grant you the cupboard where stories are kept in bottles. In return I tell you, the storyteller, to warn the whole town of the Will-o'-the-Wisp who lead people onto crooked paths." And the man agreed to tell all he met that the Will-o'-the-Wisps are in town, and the Marsh Woman bids you beware – to leave the marshes be, for the wisps and the witches are always watching!

The Night Owls

Do not get caught in the dark! This is one of the repeated messages of folklore and fairy tale. One of the creatures of the dark, the Strix, hovers in silent flight between myth, magic and the material, mortal realm. The Strix of lore is a creature of ancient Greco-Roman mythology, a vampiric bird demon or witch in night owl form, silently stalking the night skies – drinking the blood of infants as they slept and drunkards out alone at night. The word is drawn from the ancient Greek meaning 'to screech', and *strix* is the Latin word for owl (and the root of the scientific name for the owl family – Strigiformes). This was then applied to both screech owls and witch, that in classical lore are considered one and the same.

The Strix are predecessors and symbolic archetypes for the concept of both night-flying witches and vampires. The distinctive attributes of nocturnal habits, haunting calls and stealthy flight became intertwined with the mythology surrounding witches who were thought to possess the abilities of night flight.

To see Strix is an ill omen indeed. Folkloric beings inspired by the Strix can be found in various forms across southern Europe, such as the *strega* in Italy, the *striges* in Greece, and the *strigoi* in Romania. Such intertwining narratives offer a glimpse into the interplay of ancient beliefs, folkloric traditions, and the collective human fascination with the unseen and the magical that created some of our most well-known superstitions about witches.*

MONSTERS...

The wildwood has always been a place of revelation, so as we come to the end of this section, I will leave you with this: the root of the word

---

*   Every culture has images and imaginings of witch-like beings – strega, bruja, Baba Yaga, dakini, Cunning Folk – but these are not just straight translations of the word witch – every country and culture has its own unique creations of fear and trepidation in forms of powerful people connected to magic.

monster, which many of these magical dwellers of the wildwood were considered to be, is drawn from the Latin word *monere*, which means 'to show, to warn, remind or instruct' and *monstrum* 'divine omen (good and bad), portent, sign'. So, these monsters, dwellers of the wildwood, are literally demonstrative: they reveal truths, often uncomfortably so.

The Will-o'-the-Wisps and Green Ladies show us the terrible consequences of destroying the natural world, something we may all have to face in our lifetime. The violence of the Baobhan Sith and Jeanie the Bogle is so jarring, perhaps, as it is more likely to be men who senselessly attack women, and in the present day, women can still feel unsettled and fearful walking paths alone. These are true horrors of the world we live in. Perhaps all our collective trespasses against nature may be avenged one day by things we do not yet know of or can even see. That's pretty scary.

In story and lore, monstrous beings can act as reminders, warnings and bright mirrors – showing us flaws in societies and ourselves – such as how we may treat those we see as 'other' as well as making us face up to hate, arrogance, greed and jealousy. But also, the way the stories are told can show us something of the society within which they were created – for example, when stories from the ancient oral tradition of the Celts were committed to paper by Christian monks, goddesses could not be tolerated by a Christian worldview, so powerful, rebellious, complicated divine deities were reinvented, made either maidens or monsters – either repurposed as saints or cast out as witches, hags, crones, fairy women and malevolent wanderers of the wilds – because all the complexities of the in-between was too much to fathom. The misogyny of Christianity can be seen in the distorted extremes of hags and haloed saints (and perhaps in how many women in the Bible get called prostitutes).

Many of these monstrous stories serve as a dramatic reversal of the real-world power dynamics, where men have historically exerted control and dominance. The fears associated with witches and monsters often stem from the distortion of societal norms, and the projection of anxieties onto women and others who challenge the established order. Exploring these narratives can provide an opportunity to gain a richer understanding of the multifaceted roles of women, encompassing wisdom, power and the capacity to evoke fear, shedding light on the complexities of gender dynamics throughout history.

Biases can be deeply ingrained in cultural narratives, reinforcing stereotypes and prejudices. Witches, for example, often symbolise the fear of female power and sexuality, which can be projected onto individuals who don't conform to traditional gender roles. These projections reveal our insecurities and how we externalise our inner conflicts with others. And we can all, at times, struggle with those who differ from the expected roles and behaviours – and today, 'other' can still be painted as 'monster'.

The creatures of the trees may challenge our imaginations, senses and fears as embodiments of a feeling that the very wildwood itself may be watching you, or worse, plotting to do you harm, seeing you as an unwelcome intruder or disrespectful traveller. In these darkest stories, like the darkest woods, we cultivate a connection to place, untangling and revealing ideas that span history and cultures. When someone emerges from the dark of the trees of a fairytale woods, they are not the same as when they went in. It is through stories that we may find the tools we need: wonder and wisdom, imagination and enchantment, compassion for others, compassion for ourselves, courage, perseverance and understanding to navigate the woods… and our lives, as well as narratives that make sense of it all.

So, however you may feel about these 'monsters' we have met so far – witches, wild beings, and beasts – ask yourself, perhaps, what do they show to you of your own fears?

4

GODS & GODDESSES
OF THE WILDWOOD

Some see the monsters and strange figures of the wildwood as distortions of older pagan deities. Where Christian churches were built for a God, earlier pagan cultures had sacred groves, sanctuaries in the trees and deities that inhabited them. These enchanting woodlands were home to a myriad of woodland gods and goddesses, each holding sway over the natural world and the spirits that roamed within. These beings, once revered by various European cultures, represent our ancestors' deep connection with nature and the spiritual realm, leaving behind legends and folklore that continue to captivate.

The deities presented in this chapter reveal the diverse beliefs and practices of our ancestors, as well as the ever-evolving nature of folklore. Some of these figures may have once had historical roots, but the passage of time and the evolution of storytelling have transformed them into mythical beings, deities and demons, their stories interwoven with symbolism and meaning. Others have been promoted to deities in more modern literature. But whether they are remnants of ancient matriarchal societies, the guardians of sacred spaces, or the personification of natural elements, these deities continue to inspire and spark our imagination.

Not a single one of the characters we will meet in this chapter is completely benevolent; these are not visions of a 'perfect good' and inspiration – if such a thing has ever existed. But perhaps more like us as humans, they display rage, lust, ferociousness, and very often the need for dominion takes over. These are deities of the wilds after all, we may think of nature as being cruel in her storms or angry weather or merciless climates, but these deities, just like the natural world, simply display the full range of possibilities: they cannot be simplified as purely 'good' and 'bad', instead they are multi-faceted, ever-varied and unpredictable, to be considered and respected by the sensible traveller.

These are just a few of the European wood-dwelling gods and goddesses...

- The Antlered Gods of the Greenwood: Elen of the Ways (Celtic roots) and Cernunnos (Gaulish/Celtic)

- The Cailleach and her Deer herds (Scottish)

- The Huntresses: Artemis (Greek) and Diana (Roman)

- Lady of Sacred Groves: Nemetona (Celtic/Gaulish)

- Flora and Fauna, goddesses of plants and animals (Roman)

- Wild Witch Huntress: Brimo/Hecate (Greek)

- Gifts and retribution from Demeter (Greek)

- Pandemonium: Pan (Greek)

- The She-Wolf: Žvėrūna-Medeina (Lithuanian)

- The Honey-rich Mother of the Woodland: Mielikki (Finnish)

The Antlered Gods of the Greenwood

I'm not sure if any woodland figures from lore, history or fiction have quite the same draw to us here in the British Isles as the antlered deities. These figures captivate as a symbol of both the hunter and the hunted, the guardian and the destroyer. And as an elusive figure as well, the antlered god is one we see in shadows and whispers, grasping best we can to names and possible stories. As deities they are half lost, but loved, and never forgotten.

Horned deities have been worshipped throughout the ancient worlds. The Egyptian goddess Hathor has a cow horn headdress, and in some carvings Inanna, Sumerian goddess of love and war, seems to have them too. The ancient Greco-Roman deities, Pan and sometimes Bacchus/Dionysus are horned (and consistently horny, going by their most well-known mythology!). The Deer Woman of Native American mythology, Sami Goddess Beaivi, Ukrainian

Rohanitsa, and Serbian and Croatian Baba Roga, a folkloric hag figure similar to Baba Yaga, but with the addition of a horn upon her head (*rog* meaning horn) are just some global examples of deities connected to deer and with horns of varying kinds. Deer women/ women of the deer have been associated with fertility, motherhood, regeneration and the rebirth of the sun (the theme of winter solstice) from the Great Goddess to more humble folkloric hag figures. We have already seen many horns, hoofs and tails in the forest dwellers we have met so far, from the huldra to the Baobhan Sith – indicators perhaps of their wild natures, and their closer connection to the wild and *not-quite-human*-ness.

Throughout Europe we find deer and their antlers feature prominently in art from ancient carvings to headdresses,* jewellery, sacred vessels, and even tattoos found on the skin of well-preserved bog bodies. (I imagine it is no coincidence that horned and hooved beings became painted as demonic – as the Church took the most popular of pagan images and painted them as evil.) Witches were famously suspected of flying off to meet their horned master (the devil) and in folk festivities as well, where dances, rituals and plays often involved folks dressed as rams and bulls or carrying antlers. Churchmen and parishioners would attempt to ban such heathen revelry, but many practices have nonetheless persisted, or been revived. There is something primal about the strange horned and hooved half-human, half-beast that speaks deeply to us, it seems.

Elen of the Ways

Within the collection of stories known as the Mabinogion[8] is a tale called "The Dream of Macsen Wledig" in which there is a radiant woman called Elen. The character, Macsen Wledig is an emperor of Rome (it is the Welsh name for Magnus Maximus). He dreams of

---

* Excavations of the British Mesolithic site of Star Carr in the 1950's found no fewer than twenty-one headdresses made of red deer antlers.

a journey across mountains and rivers, and at the journey's end he comes upon a beautiful castle. He enters and on a golden throne sits Elen (in some translations her name is anglicised to Helen), the most beautiful woman he has ever seen, shining golden like the sun. He marries Elen and she becomes Empress Elen. The people of Britain, assembled in their love and respect for her, building great roads through the land, connecting her new and various castles, these were known as the roads of Elen of the Hosts.

Story and history can get confusing because this Elen and Magnus Maximus may have actually existed in history. Elen Luyddog (Elen of the Hosts) is thought to be a late fourth-century founder of churches in Wales, and is a saint in the Welsh Church (in English she is sometimes known as Saint Elen/Helen of Caernarfon). Roman roads on modern maps still show the 160 mile "Sarn Helen", and other Roman roads also bear Helen's name. There are also twenty or more holy wells in Britain dedicated to St. Helen, and she is acknowledged as a kind of patron of roads and pathways and a protectress and provider for travellers. These may or may not all be the same Elen/Helen.

This collective story of 'Elen' and her roads presents her as a path-making figure – both metaphorical and the literal ones. The British Isles is a land of many paths: Roman roads, ancient trackways, ley lines and animal tracks, and step by step, story by story, the pathways made by Elen in story and the pathways made by other elements – celestial pathways of sun and moon, dawn and dusk[9] and of migration of reindeer[†], roe deer and stag – all blend together in the words of storytellers and folklore. Over time, for better or worse, a woman, a story character, a saint and road infrastructure become connected to our oldest and most ancient deer goddesses. Elen becomes connected with antlered deities, and portrayed by some, as a goddess. Guardian of all travellers and journey makers.

† Red Deer, Roe Deer, Fallow, Sika and Muntjac all still live in the British Isles. But reindeer, the only species of deer in which the females have antlers, are long since extinct in the British Isles – but it means that horned deities could once represent both masculine and feminine. And the goddess form of Elen is popularly portrayed with antlers in modern artworks – possibly from female reindeer.

FINDING GODDESSES IN THE MABINOGION

This elevation of Elen, from her first written forms to a goddess, is not unique. Within the collected tales of the Mabinogion, stories weave together folklore, Celtic history and tradition and are set in a magical version of Wales. These stories evolved and developed through the Celtic and Welsh people who embellished them with each new telling. What's fascinating is that the Mabinogion – the Welsh tales retold by an English author, Lady Charlotte Guest – features no female characters described specifically as goddesses, but instead we meet powerful characters with otherworldly skills, charms and abilities such as shapeshifting, which may signify various Gallo-Brittonic deities, or gods in human form, or humans with divine abilities. Can lost goddesses be found in the Mabinogion or is it the catalyst that created new ones? We may reflect on what these enchanting characters may have meant to medieval Welsh audiences and readers (and reasons why Guest may not have specifically named pagan figures and gods – such as appeasing Christians). As the great stories are retold by bards and storytellers and artists the status of some figures may have been enhanced, even promoted to deities – or older Welsh tales may always have seen them as such.

Rhiannon, for example, is described as noble lady of the Otherworld, rather than explicitly a goddess. But this connection to the Otherworld and royalty suggests she may have been a pagan goddess figure or fairy queen. Cerridwen is a mother skilled in sorcery, shapeshifting and the brewing of potions in the Mabinogion (a woman many would call a witch) and in 1809 clergyman and antiquarian Edward Davies deemed her a goddess of ancient Britain in his *Mythology & Rites of British Druids* (an identity accepted by many since). Gwyn ap nudd in eleventh and twelfth century texts is one of King

Arthur's warriors. In time poets would make him a lord of the Underworld, and he becomes a spirit of darkness and deception. Then Sir John Rhys, an Oxford professor writing around 1880s, crowned him a Celtic god of the dead and yet another leader of the Wild Hunt (many beings, deities and spirits took on this role in varied stories). These transformations may irk scholars, but are a gift to artists, writers and all folks inspired by the stories, maybe there's a little magic in these tales that can't be quantified, and a fine story…even the deities can't suppress those!

Elen has somewhat been reborn in modern times as an antlered goddess who rules the Ways: the passages of human life, both physical and spiritual. And so, we arrive at a path-making, goddess of guidance figure in Elen of the Ways. The marrying of the name Elen of the Ways and goddess figure with antlers was very recent (around the 1980s). Caroline Wise devoted decades into research of ancient antlered deities and wrote about Elen as goddess in *Elen of the Shimmering Ways* in 1986. As with many modern pagan/wiccan ideas, some are newer than others, but most have ancient roots.

So now, when one says "Elen of the Ways", many see an ancient goddess, the soul of the forest, creator of tracks and paths, guide to human and animal movement over the wild places. A goddess whose favour may be sought in travelling, making one's way, connected to the land and its rhythms, its ancient forms and slow changes. She can be a representative of our many lost ancient deities with horns and hooves, who assists us in connecting to the animals and the land. Some call her Elen of the Ways, some don't, but if something here resonates, it might be that this figure offers us a feeling of guidance and protection, so often missing in our modern lives. Perhaps this lady of the wildwood has no care for what you try to name her, she who is hidden amongst the trees; only the lucky few may catch a glimpse before she slips silently amongst ancient branches once more.

Cernunnos

Another mysterious antlered figure is Cernunnos. Despite his contemporary popularity in books and oracle decks, there are no recorded myths or ancient literary sources that directly reference Cernunnos. He, where we see him depicted, is a mysterious horned figure often surrounded by animals, sometimes portrayed with wild hair and beard and with mighty antlers, as most likely, a god of beasts and wild places. The name Cernunnos is drawn from a carved name relief found underneath the Cathedral of Notre-Dame at Paris. The carved stone displays various Gallic and Greco-Roman deities, including the horned god thought to be a representation of this deity. Antlered god icons can be found in various artefacts; the Gundestrup cauldron of Denmark is a well-known example of a horned deity that is often called Cernunnos. While we have little idea of what these varied depictions of antlered figures were called and what specific deities they represented, Cernunnos is the assumed Celtic/Gaulish name and it has pervaded the English-speaking world. So, Cernunnos (meaning "horned" or "horned one") has become the name for a kind of amalgam of many horned gods, woodland deities, and hunter imagery. We will meet more later in this chapter.

The Cailleach and Deer Women

Now to another goddess from Celtic lands, but this time from the Highlands and Islands of Scotland. Here the red deer of the mountains were known as the "cattle of the Cailleach", the crone goddess who brings forth the winter and dark half of the year. The Cailleach has many embodiments, including protectress of wild things and as a deer goddess tending her herds of deer in Glen Nevis. The Isle of Jura derived its name from Norse, meaning 'deer isle', so called, some say, because of the seven deer-goddesses or giantesses who lived there with their herds.

The deer as a symbol was important in ancient belief in Scotland.

Deer were sacred creatures, symbolising connections to the divine and otherworld. Scottish folklore is rich with stories and legends featuring mystical and mysterious deer – it is often said that a deer may well lead humans into the realm of the fairies. Deer hunting was a popular sport among the Scottish aristocracy, so the animals were also symbols of strength and nobility, qualities that passed onto the hunters that successfully pursued them. But even hunters of the deer should treat them with respect...

In the east of Scotland, the Cailleach is also known as the Carlin. In various regions, she is called *Cailleach Mhor nam Fiadh* (Big Carlin of the Deer) or *Cailleach Beinn a' Bhric* (Carlin of Ben Breck), who is known by some as a giantess and by others as a goddess and as a protector of deer. She may well help the deer to escape death from the hunter. She may appear as an old woman, hence her Cailleach/Carlin title, but sometimes she's younger and even shapeshifts into a deer herself. If she appears as a deer, she may change back if the hunter raises his gun to try to shoot her. And she may reprimand hunters for killing too many of her hinds. Other faerie or bewitched women may also appear as deer in Scottish folklore. Stories about Cailleach Beinn a' Bhric are told throughout the Highlands and Islands, and folk songs and poems may tell of the Cailleach singing while she roamed the glens as a spirit, protecting the deer.

In the 1930's J.G. McKay put forward his theories on matriarchal societies and deer-cults of Scotland. Inspired by Gaelic tales of wild feminine characters, who appeared as such figures as fairy women, witches and giantesses, who owned, herded, and milked deer (and the fact that he considered all women to be a bit magical...).

"Long, long ago, a state of society existed in the Highlands,
when woman was supreme; all women were supernatural
and magical; all ghosts whether of male or female creatures
were feminine; fairyland of the Otherworld, was tenanted or
inhabited by exclusively women; men were in the hunting stage
of development and feared women, their spiritual mothers, all

*of whom were capable of guiding the destinies of men magically,
either for their weal or woe, as they chose; the deer was a god;
the ghosts of deer became fairy or supernatural women; and
deer were the cattle of the fairies or of supernatural beings.*"

**J. G. McKay, *The Deer-Cult and the Deer-Goddess Cult of the
Ancient Caledonians* (1932)**

TREE-TALES: BLACKTHORN (PRUNUS SPINOSA)

In some Celtic and Gaelic stories, the Cailleach, the Celtic
queen of winter, carries a blackthorn stick. The crone goddess moves across winter mountains, driving and safeguarding
her beloved herds of wild cattle and deer with her blackthorn
staff. If the winter goddess is slow to depart in spring, and cold
weather is still present when the blackthorn is flowering, that
is known as a "blackthorn winter." Folk names for blackthorn
include Sloe Plum, Wishing Thorn, Mother of the Woods, the
Dark Crone of the Woods (likely from her connections to the
Cailleach), and Faery Tree.

In Irish mythology, the blackthorn tree was home to fairies.
If you cut one down, they could wreak havoc upon you. In
The Fairy-Faith in Celtic Countries (1911), Dr Evans-Wentz
tells a beautiful story of the *Lunantisidhe* (Lunantishee) moon
fairies who inhabit and guard the blackthorns of Ireland. The
dark fruit of the blackthorn (sloes) are the sweetest harvested
after a frost; and the best time to harvest sloes is on the full
moon nights of midwinter for this is when the *Lunantisidhe*
fairies have left the tree to visit the moon goddess. Sloes are
popular for creating drinks and jams, they also act as an as-
tringent, making them popular naturopathic medicine to re-
duce inflammation – so herbalists and witches have used them
in remedies and foodstuffs since time immemorial.

Classical Goddesses of the Forest

In the deep recesses of the wildwoods, ancient deities come alive, illustrating the power of human imagination to give life to forces that both inspire awe and instil fear. They remind us that the wild, though formidable and unpredictable, is an intrinsic part of our existence, and in contemplating these divine figures, we recognise that our journey into the wilds is not solely an exploration of the external realm, but an introspective voyage into something within ourselves. Just as the ancient worshippers found solace and wisdom in the embrace of these deities, so too can we draw inspiration from their myths. Each deity shows different aspects of the natural world and how we, as societies have viewed our relationship with it.

These figures offer us a glimpse into the ancient understanding of the natural world as a sacred realm, where the spirits of gods and goddesses reside, and where humans could seek guidance, protection, favour and connection to the forces of nature. Today, as we encounter these mythical beings through folklore and ancient texts, we are reminded of the deep reverence our ancestors held for the wildwood and a world where the veil between the seen and the unseen was thin, and where nature and spirituality were intertwined.

Artemis

In ancient Greece, Artemis was the goddess of wild animals, the hunt and woodland, particularly popular among the rural people who could see her realm all around them. Sculptors, poets and painters portrayed Artemis almost universally as a young, beautiful huntress carrying a quiver with arrows and holding a bow, accompanied by a stag, doe or hunting dogs. As a moon goddess, she may be seen wearing a crescent moon crown, her gown is made of the very shadows and mists of the wilds, and she dwells in the deepest forests where men cannot go.

She is also considered a protector of women, and in story, more than one male character has tried to dishonour Artemis, few of them lived past their poor choices.

When the king of Calydon fails to honour the goddess, she sends a giant wild boar to wreak havoc on his kingdom. In the hunting party to kill the boar it is a huntress, Atlanta, who draws first blood. This causes outrage in the hunting men, which results in even more chaos and death: a further reminder to the men of Calydon and beyond who hear the tale not to disrespect women or goddesses.

When the hunter Actaeon walks into a sacred grove of pines and cypress where a waterfall falls into a clear pool, he sees Artemis bathing naked.* As punishment she transforms him into a stag and sets his hounds against him, ripping him apart. Like many classical goddesses, Artemis is certainly not to be disrespected or trifled with.

Diana

In the ancient Roman pantheon, Diana, like Artemis, is the goddess of nature, wild animals, women, woodland and the hunt. She was also associated with hunting hounds and deer, and connected with their qualities of strength and instincts, gracefulness and agility. Near Rome, at Lake Nemi, a temple complex that once covered an area of 45,000 square metres (but is now ruins) was a famed place of worship for the goddess – the grove of Diana Nemorensis (Diana of the Wood).

This would have been where the festival of Nemoralia was held in honour of Diana and her sacred groves, with torch-lit festivities, devotions and gifts offered on the August Full Moon. Parties in the shaded woods would be both a chance to honour Diana as well as es-

---

* The fable of Actaeon was a popular one and many versions can be found including ones featuring Diana, a Roman goddess wildly similar to Artemis, in some versions of the story Actaeon accidentally comes across the goddess, in others he uses a stag's pelt to sneak up on her and some where he is torn apart for boasting to be a better hunter than the goddess.

cape from the city and the heat of the Lion's Sun (the star sign of Leo is in the sky through July and August). The Nemoralia was a festival rejoicing in the many facets of Diana, Goddess of the Wilds and its beasts, the moon, guardian of the trees and their resident nymphs. The festival was also known as the Festival of Torches because worshippers assembled by torch or candlelight at Lake Nemi. They also assembled in special rituals of washing their hair before dressing it with flowers. Dogs, Diana's hunting companions, were also honoured and likewise adorned with flowers. Worshippers wrote prayers and wishes upon ribbons, which were then tied to trees. Sacrifices were made of fruits and icons baked in bread, such as miniature stags and female figures. Hunting was forbidden during the festival (presumably to give Diana free reign for her favourite sport), and women were free from their homely duties to celebrate the goddess.

Though these celebrations started at Lake Nemi, they soon spread through Roman territories as the empire grew, and expanded to celebrate sacred wild places – water, groves and woods and unspoiled nature – these being the liminal spaces, those separating wild from civilised, but also the living from dead, where deities are best found.

In her connections to wild nature and women, Diana is named as leader of the procession that would become known as the Wild Hunt, and we see her become more demonic in Christian eyes.

THE WILD HUNT

The term 'Wild Hunt' is one of many names for assemblies of spirits who journey through the night sky in Western culture, ever since German folklorist Jacob Grimm wrote of "The Wild Hunt" of Odin and Holda in his book *Deutsche Mythologie* (1835). Grimm's ideas were, perhaps, so well received in Britain and Europe because of a pre-existing interest and popular stories of ghostly huntsmen, flying nocturnal females and phantom hounds.*

Who better to lead a hunt than a huntress and goddess of women and their wild nature, Diana?

A collection of texts of canon law of the Catholic Church from 900-1000CE contain some fascinating stories of night riding women, and the goddess Diana.

"Some wicked women...seduced by illusions and phantasms of demons, believe and profess that, in the hours of the night, they ride upon certain beasts with Diana, the goddess of the pagans, and an innumerable multitude of women, and in the silence of the night traverse great spaces of earth..."[†]

This text was tweaked over the years, and the story of night flying hordes of witches is repeated and retold in many texts. The procession described in the *Canon Episcopi* is one version of old tales that may well have played a part in future myths of the witches' sabbath[‡] – which was often mentioned in trials accusing 'witches' of malevolence. And whilst these 'wicked women' are not necessarily the foundations for what was later

---

* Further British variants include the additions of specific phantom hounds who run with spectral packs; the Whisht Hounds (Melancholy) of Devon and Somerset, the Yell or Yeth (Heath) Hounds, Wish or Witch Hounds of Sussex. There are also the Fairy Rides of Scotland who hunt unwary humans to drag into the otherworld.

† After taking such care with this tantalising description, the Canon notes that this is all illusion/superstition, which is rather a shame... According to the Canon Episcopi – the Church's official viewpoint – witches and magic did not exist, but the devil did – and could possess the minds of the susceptible female and any who actually believed themselves to be a witch were dreaming or delusional. Views on magic and witchcraft began to shift during the Middle Ages, leading to witches being very real in the eyes of many, real enough to be hunted, tortured and killed.

‡ Also called conviviums, conventicles, assemblies, black sabbaths and witches sabbaths.

named the Wild Hunt, and all the many cultural variations of night flying hunters are not necessarily literally connected, they are certainly flying under some similar themes, and we can enjoy the commonality of such stories that clamber out of wild weather or deep dark nights.

Nemetona

Celtic Gaulish[§] goddess Nemetona is an ancient goddess connected to sacred groves. Celtic tribes designated and tended nemetons, or sacred groves, in the clearings of forests. These were hallowed spaces where one could connect to or communicate with deities. And so, the theory is that Nemetona was thought to be protective of the sacred spaces and their connection to divine beings. Her name may derive from the Celtic root *nemeto* referring to a sacred space, particularly sacred groves, so to many, in the modern day she is seen as a guardian goddess: She of the Sacred Grove or a Lady of Sanctuary.

Nemetona's name can be found in my hometown of Bath, England, where an ancient altar to her is dedicated (along with her consort Loucetius Mars[¶]), at the Roman Baths Museum. This suggests that she could have been honoured in tribes of Europe and journeyed with travellers to Aquae Sulis in the Roman era or that she was drawn from Roman ideas relating to forest goddesses such as Diana. Like many an ancient goddess, she now exists only in fragments. So many of our ideas about Nemetona are educated guesswork. Rituals to appease gods and seek victory in battle would have been amongst

§   Gaul was a region of Europe first described by the Romans, inhabited by Celtic tribes, encompassing present-day France, Belgium, Luxembourg, and parts of Switzerland, Italy, and Germany.

¶   Loucetius Mars, like Sulis Minerva, is an amalgam of a Celtic-Gaulish and Roman deity. The name Loucetius means 'light', so it is possible that this Mars is connected with healing through connections of light with the sun, or something a little more wild such as lightning.

the rituals performed in sacred groves, and so perhaps that is why Nemetona is connected, in at least one ancient engraving, to the war god Mars.

Flora and Fauna

If Diana and Artemis are wardens of the wildwood, we may also mention Flora and Fauna as Roman deities associated with nature and wildlife. Flora as the divine embodiment of plants and blossoming flowers, a goddess of abundance, symbol of the beauty and fertility of the natural world. Her festival, the Floralia, was once held between the end of April and the beginning of May and symbolised the renewal of the cycle of life.

The Roman goddess Fauna is deity of fruitfulness and prophecy with the woodlands, fields and the animals found there. As goddess of wildlife and animals, she also represented the untamed, wild aspects of nature. Her male counterpart was Faunus, a Roman god of the forest, fields and rural life. As a woodland deities, the sounds of the forest were thought to be Fauna/Faunus' voice, and signs may be read through the forests for those who know nature's omens.

Together, Flora and Fauna personify the interconnectedness of plant and animal life in the natural environment, the essence of the living world. They may be lesser-known deities in terms of written myth, but we still use their names today, flora and fauna refer to the collective plant life and animal life of a region.

Witch Goddess Brimo/Hecate

The Greco-Roman myths and legends significantly contributed to our modern-day images and archetypes of witches – Circe, Hecate, Medea, Canidia – avenging goddesses and women all found at times in wild places.

Circe lived on Aeaea, an island of lush forests and animals. In "Rhizotomoi" (Root Cutters), the playwright Sophocles (496-406 BCE) describes sorceress and healer Medea, naked and chanting as she collects the salves seeping from roots of plants sliced open with her bronze sickle. And Roman poet Horace (65-8 BCE) draws on the myths and traditions of witchcraft – Medea's potions, Circe's spells, and Hecate's place in the Underworld – to create the image of human witch Canidia:

> *"Canidia, having entwined her hair and uncombed head*
> *with tiny snakes, commands wild fig-tree grubbed up from*
> *graves, commands funereal cypresses, and the eggs besmeared*
> *with the gore of a venomous toad, and plumage of a midnight*
> *screech-owl, and herbs, which Iolcos and Iberia, fertile in*
> *poisons produce, and the bones snatched from the mouth*
> *of a famished bitch, to be burnt in Colchian fires."*

Along with this evocative witch imagery, Greco-Roman myths gave us the harpies, gorgons, sirens and furies. Men have long been making beasts and monsters of women, with ancient texts painting them as hysterical, devious, vicious, cunning and unclean – it's enough to make anyone a fury, which brings us to the witch-goddess Brimo-Hecate:

> *"And over the gateway sits Brimo, the wild witch-huntress*
> *of the woods, brandishing a pine-torch in her hands, while*
> *her mad hounds howl around. No man dare meet her*
> *or look on her, but only I her priestess, and she watches*
> *far and wide lest any stranger should come near"*

William Patten, *Tales from Greece and Rome* (1912)

In the story of the Argonauts, the sorceress Medea helps Jason and his crew evade Brimo to retrieve the golden fleece. Medea knows

Brimo to be an incarnation of the goddess Hecate and she feeds raw meat strewn with herbs and honey to the witch of the woods and her wild hounds so that our heroes may enter her realm – the poison woods – to retrieve the golden fleece from the vast tree it hangs on. Medea is known in most stories as both sorceress and a priestess of the goddess Hecate, so she treats Brimo with reverence and respect. Brimo means 'angry' or 'terrifying', and in the "Argonautica", Hecate is also described as Brimo, in her most fearsome underworld form, a formidable being who expresses primal, screaming rage. Crowned with venomous snakes and oak branches, in her wake, the ground shakes, and from her footsteps grow the most poisonous flowers and roots.

In ancient Greek religion and myth, the moniker "Brimo" may be applied to several goddesses with fearful and vengeful aspects that are linked to the underworld: Persephone, Demeter, the Erinyes/Furies to name a few. (Many cultures use this dual aspect of goddesses to show their dual sides of nurturer and destroyer.)

> *"Now she had gathered for her drugs the dark juice thereof,*
> *like to the sap of a mountain oak, in a Caspian shell, after*
> *she had washed herself in seven eternal springs, and seven*
> *times had called on Brimo, good nursing-mother, who*
> *roams by night, goddess of the nether world, and queen of*
> *the dead, in the murk of night, in sable raiment clad. And,*
> *from beneath, the dark earth quaked and bellowed."*

Apollonius Rhodius, "Argonautica" (300 BCE)

Demeter Avenges her Sacred Grove

This is another tale of revenge for human greed and disrespect. This time featuring Demeter, a prominent goddess in Greek mythology, revered as the deity of agriculture, harvest and fertility. The mother of Persephone, Demeter, is the creatrix of changing seasons: her grief over her daughter's abduction by Hades and descent into the Underworld each autumn, and joy at Persephone's return each spring, causes the cycle of the seasons on Earth. This tale illustrates the power of human arrogance, but most of all greed and the horrors it can create if it becomes all-consuming (which it does literally in this tale). Greed and arrogance are the downfall of many humans in traditional tales and the gods serve as agents of retribution and warning. The story also speaks to a necessity of respecting the sacred feminine and Mother Earth – a warning still essential for humans today.

In ancient Greece, it is said there once lived a king whose name was Erysichthon. He was foolish and arrogant. One morning Erysichthon wanted to prove that there existed no gods, so all should worship him and him alone. So, he journeyed to a grove of trees sacred to the goddess Demeter.

In the centre of the grove, there was an ancient oak. When blades struck the trees, dark blood poured from the bark and howling cries came from the tree. The king was undeterred and laughed as the trees crashed to the ground. That night the nymphs wept around the desecrated grove.

Demeter would have her revenge. She sent for the spirit of Hunger. And that night, Hunger flew through the sky to the palace of King Erysichthon and, with a kiss, blew a torrent of starvation into his open mouth.

The following day, when the king woke, he found his jaws

had a life of their own. He called for food. He ate and ate, but his hunger was like fire: the more he fed it, the stronger it became. He called for more, food enough to feed his city; he crammed into his open mouth. He only stopped chewing to call for "More food! More food!" He ate his way through all his wealth. He sold all his lands, herds, and properties until, at last, he sold his daughter into slavery for a meal. (Demeter granted her a moment of invisibility to escape.)

But a worse fate yet met the hungry king. One day, in his eagerness to eat, he bit into his finger, then his hand and King Erysichthon eventually devoured himself completely.

Pan

Could the true fear lurking in the forest depths originate from a realm deeper and darker than the tales of folklore? Perhaps it resides within the domain of deities, a place more akin to the Underworld, where an obscure essence of otherness exists – somewhere beyond, beneath, and betwixt. Here, we encounter primal instincts that can prove challenging to restrain, but are looked at with disdain from 'civilised' society and religions such as Christianity: desire, rage and greed. It's noteworthy that the word 'panic' finds its roots in the fear and unleashed chaos brought forth by the Greek god Pan, whose domain encompasses the unruly wilderness, woods and forests.

As god of the wild, Pan is suitably made up of legs and horns of a goat, and found in the shaded groves and wooded glens rather than the bright marble courts of Olympus. As a god, Pan was worshipped (and feared) in ancient times. In more recent eras, Romantic poets saw the god Pan as a representative of the wild and dangerous elements of nature. Pan embodied the mysteries of the natural world. Part god, part goat – fertile, powerful, sometimes dangerous and instigator of terror within the beauty of the woods and of wild chaos. It is no wonder, then, the similarities drawn between Pan and depictions of the Devil in Christianity, both possess the spirit of 'otherness' that seems to result in, and inspire, immoral behaviours.

GODDESSES FROM NORTHERN EUROPEAN FOLKLORE

Žvėrūna-Medeina

Lithuanian forest deity, ruler of forests, trees and animals, in texts, she is alternately called both Medeina and Žvorūna or paired as Žvėrūna-Medeina. Both names are related to hunting, Žvorūna, drawn from *žvėris* (beast), referring to a hunting hound or she-wolf, and Medeina is related to the trees. Comparable to both Artemis and Diana in her depictions as a beautiful huntress and young woman, she is also depicted as a she-wolf with an accompanying pack of wolves. She is also connected to hares, and folk beliefs suggest that hares helped the goddess protect her forests, especially by leading hunters astray. Hunters may fear seeing a hare in Žvėrūna-Medeina's forests and may not hunt on any day that one is sighted. The first kill of the year may be sacrificed to Žvėrūna-Medeina, and offerings proffered for the protection of domestic animals from her wolves.

Again, like Artemis and Diana, her duty is not necessarily to help hunters (though she does occasionally) but to protect the forest. Followers revered her, and places known as Hare Churches (sacred stones, hills, forests) and wolf footprints (stones with hollows that resemble a footprint) have been identified by archaeologists in the wild spaces of Eastern Lithuania[10] inspired by this goddess.

Mielikki

Mielikki is the mistress and mother of woodland in Finnish lore. Goddess of the hunt and wild animals – bears in particular – she represents luck, abundance and healing. Mielikki is connected to beauty and elegance for she makes the forest beautiful; woodland flowers, autumnal leaves, the elegant shapes of the trees are all thanks to her. She is referred to in various tales as connected by family or marriage to Tapio, the forest god, who may be represented as very tall with a foliate beard, coat of tree moss and crown of fir twigs. Both Tapio and Mielikki were shapeshifters and could turn themselves into trees and bears. Mielikki and her family of forest deities were held in high reverence, and stories tell of their wooden castle deep in the heart of the forest where they are served upon by nature spirits and forest elves and watch over their wild animals.

Mielikki is called in "The Kalevala", the Finnish national epic, "The Honey-rich Mother of the Woodland" and "The Hostess of the Glen and Forest."[11] It was thought she held the keys to the forest's treasures, including great chests of honey (the food of the forest deities and treasured treat of weary hunters.) Her name is thought to be derived from the old Finnish word *mielu*, which means luck, and hunters and foragers alike might entreat the goddess with prayers and offerings for her favour and luck when hunting and seeking berries, nuts, honey and mushrooms in the forest. In a country where the forest was central to providing food through hunting and gathering, it was very important to stay on her good side. When the hunters were successful, she was represented as beautiful and benign, her hands glittering with gold and silver ornaments and wearing garlands of pearls. However, when the hunt was unsuccessful, she was described as a hideous, dressed in tattered clothes.

Like many goddesses Mielikki had dual roles as wild huntress and also the healing mother goddess. As healer, Mielikki might heal the paws of animals that had escaped traps, rescue chicks fallen from their nests and treat the wounds of fighting animals such as deer.

She knows well the healing herbs, and, as well as aiding animals in distress throughout the forest, humans who knew her well enough could also ask for help. She was worshipped by many, particularly healers who practised herbal magic.

ANCIENT AND MODERN

There are lost figures, faded deities, people of the wild in our past that recur again and again in theme and story – the horned man, the stag, the old woman. You may jump in and name them with the titles you know – Cernunnos, Elen of the Ways, Cailleach – but the truth is, we know very little about these ancient deities. Both Elen of the Hosts/Ways and Cernunnos are examples of where a name has been found (in text and carving respectively) and grasped as suitable for deities whose names have been lost to time. This doesn't make the names wrong, similar to the case of the Green Man, all three have come to be known widely by these names, because, as with many ancient deities, we are working with only faint traces and remains from oral cultures.

This highlights an interesting point about folklore – we as individuals do not get to decide, what stories endure; all we can do is share the ones that speak to us and revel in the journey of listening and remembering. For example, not everyone can get enthusiastic about the enduring image of lascivious god Pan who pursued nymphs to such an extent they turned themselves into trees and plants to escape him (Pitys and Syrinx respectively). Not everyone likes the way Lady Raglan grouped together and titled foliate heads and festival figures "The Green Man", or the more modern naming of figures who may or may not have been goddesses, like Elen of the Ways. And yet, these images seem to capture folks' imaginations and get carried away into a lore of their own: used to create new stories and narratives, becoming figureheads for social justice and spiritual defenders of wild places. This is folklore in action, as it continues to journey through time as a living presence, such is the power of a good story: it speaks to the deep and ancient places within and without and connects us to them and each other.

5

REAL WITCHES OF
THE WILDWOOD

The archetype of the witch in the woods has long been etched into our collective consciousness through myths and legends. We met her as children in fairy tales, and ancient civilisations saw witch-like figures in the wilds and in-between realms. Her figure was hewn from story, superstitions, and she was/ is a connection to older rural and herbal practices that are the root of all our modern medicines and science.

Now, we step beyond the realm of fiction (or rather, have one foot in each category as these stories often involve a bit of both), as we discover that this enduring archetype of the witch in the woods finds echoes in the lives of real women who have chosen to immerse themselves in the wilderness or to protect and preserve the natural world. We'll encounter a range of real women and men, who, across history, have been intrinsically linked to the wilds and its mysteries – some who claimed the name of witch proudly, and those who were branded with that title by the accusations of others.

There is no finite list of what counts as witchcraft, it is subjective, and will be different from person to person, culture to culture but can well include: working with unseen forces, divination, healing or harming with herbs and plants, casting spells, performing non-Christian ritual, making charms and curses, predicting or changing the weather, causing death or illness...

WITCHES ON TRIAL

The witch trials pinpointed certain women as 'outsiders' – perhaps those who spent too long in the wild, outside of the village or outside of Christian norms – as potentially threatening, violent and harmful. Women were considered particularly vulnerable to the attentions of the devil because they were the savage and sinful daughters of Eve. It was believed that it was only via the devil that women could be more powerful, skilled or knowledgeable than patriarchal society would like. The witchcraft persecutions could definitely be viewed as part of a distrust of any power held by women – even the modest (but essential) rule of the home and child rearing and rural arts of foraging food, herbs and healing plants. We may view witchcraft persecution as a part of a bid to control and assert power over women. Suspicions rose and lines blurred in people's minds between having the skill to find medicine in the forest and poisons.

It seems that almost any skill, possession or characteristic could be turned into the mark of a witch, and almost any activities in the home or out of it could be distorted into potential witchcraft; it certainly seems like one couldn't win. A nurturing nature may have extended to caring for animals, which also made people targets for witch accusations. The simple act of keeping animals to chase mice or guard livestock was, once again, twisted and distorted into some kind of evil act. The suspicions of witches and animal familiars, popular in British witch trials, reveal the perception of women's relationships with animals as inherently suspect. Women who shared bonds with animals were often accused of using them to perform magical acts – simple acts of feeding and caring for animals became twisted into witches controlling them to perform malefic acts or transforming into them to cause havoc; elaborate fictions used to address/explore these acts that were seen as stepping outside the boundaries of what society deemed acceptable for women.

Over the course of the late sixteenth and seventeenth century in England, the impact of the witch hysteria resulted in the publication of illustrated witchcraft pamphlets through London's printing houses, where news of witch trials would be recounted in detail. Witchcraft pamphlets often portrayed female witches as caricatures representing the believed malicious capabilities of witches where elements of folklore and superstition were presented as facts. The testimonies of accused witches, already distorted by torture may be twisted again for more sensational reading. Depictions of female witches in particular was as ugly hags. A (some might say still present in modern day) suggestion of society that women thought ugly, old, possessing of undesirable features like a large nose or loud voice, or in some way deformed (there something 'different' about them, like the Baobhan Sith's hooves), were definitely bad news and evil doers, and to many somewhat less than human. Witches were often described using various terms that emphasised their wild or animal-like nature. And we see words like feral, wild, monstrous, untamed and savage.

> *"That there were such Creatures as Witches*
> *he made no doubt at all."*

A tryal of witches, at the Assizes held at Bury St. Edmonds for the County of Suffolk, on the tenth day of March 1664

Often those accused of being witches were thought more like wild animals than humans. Making them less human may have helped justify what was done to them. These "creatures", "wretched, perillous waspes", "monsters" and "beasts" – accused witches seem grouped with existing fears of the uncivilised wilds and the creatures that lurked in the land itself with this kind of language. Common superstition had witches capable of becoming wild animals including: cats, hares, snakes, owls, dogs, birds, foxes, frogs, toads, bats and tending to them as familiars, this is just another way that witches (and those accused as such) were made beastly.

In the records of accused witch from Fife, Lilias Adie, we find that her ordeal didn't end after death. In 1852 a party from Torryburn dug up Lilias's remains, on the orders of "celebrated local antiquarian" Joseph Neil Paton, and presented him with her skull for his private collection. He called her remains animal-like, apparently "rather below than above a middle size, with the animal preponderating very much over the intellectual or moral region…but we suppose that this was an indispensable feature in the physiognomy of the whole sisterhood of witches…" (From an account of the trial and exhumation in *Fife Herald,* 13 May 1852.)

And in one final, horrible example, we need only look at the artefact of the scold's bridle, also called a witch's bridle or gossip's bridle ("scold", "witch" and "gossip" were all words commonly used to dehumanise and belittle women) to demonstrate that women were seen as, and treated as, animals. It is essentially a horse's bridle created for women, made of iron, with torturous additions such as spikes to pierce the tongue, explicitly created to control, silence, humiliate, and cause pain. Some accused of the crime of witchcraft were made to wear the bridle, other women were simply guilty, as the name suggests, of speaking out of turn. Though technically illegal in many areas, nevertheless, these devices were employed in Britain and Europe by local magistrates, from around the 1500s into the 1800s, as part of a broader culture of fear and punishment of women, used to punish those who refused conventions, and to ensure that women played the part of silent submissive wives.

Looking at accounts of real events and real people during the witch trials always proves to be both fascinating and horrifying all at once. And you'll see that the myth of the women in the wildwoods isn't quite as vivid in these real tales, but more slivers of elements that would become parts of myths and superstitions. There were, for example, no bands of women brewing from great cauldrons in the darkest hearts of forests, or women disguised as wolves, but there would no doubt have been feasts in remote tumbledown cottages, women who passed through forests, and many using charms and healing balms drawn from woods.

Written evidence of 'real witches' is sparse and hugely biased – so other sources can be useful, I will do my best to discern women's voices and agency in witch trial material, though their voices are distorted by leading questions, incomplete accounts and torture. I seek to share their names, so that we may bear witness to those being accused and what their lives and skills really looked like. Again, this is a challenge; with an absence of true first-hand accounts, I must gather stories from all realms – superstition, folklore, fairy tale – they all tell parts of a larger story – to reflect on how we once saw witches, how we see them now, and how the natural world plays a part in the tale. I am sure some scholarly historians may accuse me of over-romanticising these accused witches, but I am confident that many, if not all of them, were far wiser and valuable people than their accusers believed or they are given credit for now. The accused witch and their work were often overlooked, dismissed and belittled (as is still the case with much of the work of women in general and those in caring roles) the injustice women and witches have seen is vast and infuriating.

CUNNING FOLK AND WYRTCUNNING

In Old English "wyrtcunning" means plant knowledge; you could liken it to modern day herbalism. This was very much everyday magic and healing. Once, it wasn't a case of whether people 'believed' in it, it was simply what was there: a trust in the land and nature. You have only to look at old texts to see recipes that whisper 'spells' and 'witch' to our modern sensibilities – making 'witchy ways' simply echoes of rural/pagan/druidic/heathen ways painted as backwards or malicious to modern and Christian eras. For example, in *Bald's Leechbook* you'll find recipes for vapour and herb baths prescribed for all manner of ailments as well as 'smoke' for sick animals and humans with fragrant woods and dried herbs. *"For sunburn boil in butter tender ivy twigs, smear therewith."*

The *Lacnunga** holds over a thousand herbal remedies within its pages, one of the best known is the "Nine Herbs Charm", which involves the preparation of nine plants as a treatment against poison and infection. The charm is sung three times

*　　Some of the oldest surviving English herbal healing manuscripts are the Anglo-Saxon *Bald's Leechbook* and a medical compilation known as *Lacnunga*, both written about 900-950 CE and rooted firmly in the land and Classical and European herbal traditions.

over each of the herbs and to the patient. This reflects a wisdom that it's not just the body that is part of the healing process: charms and incantations may help the mind and spirit too.

"Now these nine herbs have power against nine magic outcasts against nine venoms and against nine flying things."

Magical ideas are interwoven through these texts including prayers and invocations from both pagan and Christian origins. It's the remnant of practices such as these, in addition to knowledge that was passed down through the generations of herbs, plants and trees that made this rural, magic-tinged practice of folk medicine.

In medieval into early modern times, rural living conditions were poor and life could be cut short by minor injuries, Doctors were scarce and expensive, and for members of Europe's lower classes, local healers were often the only option. In the British Isles, we knew these people as "cunning folk" – professional practitioners (both male and female) of folk magic from the medieval period onward who charged for their skills and services that might include: counselling, divining fortunes, treating ailments, and creating charms for healing. They might also, depending on who you spoke to, be called, either by themselves or others – witches, wise women, healers and magicians. Some may have held respected positions in the community in an age when women otherwise had little status, and others, like Chattox and Demdike who we'll meet shortly, were seemingly held in disdain for their work. The history of folk medicine is entwined with myths, folk tales, fairy tales, and the homespun magic of these cunning folk.

The witch, in some sense always dwells at the edges – whether that is physically, as the Pendle witches did out in the wilds of Pendle Forest, or marked out or seen as different, as the Torsåker forest witches were thought of. Of those accused of witchcraft some have lived on the edges of civilised society, others found themselves simply in forests in the wrong place at the wrong time. And some embraced the wilderness, settled in the forest and/or fought passionately to protect it. From the depths of ancient forests to the frontlines of environmental activism, the wild spirit of these women has left deep-rooted marks in our stories. There is an enduring legacy of these remarkable women, who, in different ways, have embodied the enigma of the witch in the woods.

THE PENDLE WITCHES

The wild stories of witches from the forests of Pendle, Lancaster, in the north of England, intertwine between history, superstitions and folk tales.

"In 1633 we find that Pendle Forest was still of bad repute, and that traditions of old Demdike and her rival Mother Chattox yet floated round the Malkin Tower, and hid, spectre-like, in the rough and desert places of the barren waste..."

Court clerk Thomas Potts's account of the proceedings, from *The Wonderfull Discoverie of Witches in the Countie of Lancaster* (1613)[12]

"It was in the lonely forest of Pendle among the wild hills of eastern Lancashire that there lived two hostile families headed by Elizabeth Southerns, or "Old Demdike," and by Anne Chattox. The latter was a wool carder, "a very old, withered, spent, and decreped creature," "her lippes ever chattering"; the former a

blind beggar of four-score years, "a generall agent for the Devell
in all these partes," and a "wicked fire-brand of mischiefe," who
had brought up her children and grandchildren to be witches.
Both families professed supernatural practices. Both families no
doubt traded on the fear they inspired. Indeed Dame Chattox
was said to have sold her guarantee to do no harm in return
for a fixed annual payment of "one aghen-dole of meale."

Wallace Notestein, *A History of Witchcraft in England from*
1558 to 1718 **(1909)**

In March 1612, a young, very poor woman was walking through
woodland from Pendle Hill. Her name was Alizon Device. The Device family were well known in the area for offering traditional herbal remedies and good luck charms, and so, of course, they were also
known as witches. When she passed by a pedlar named John Law,
one version of the story is that she asked him for some pins. He
refused (one imagines not particularly politely), and Alizon became
angry and responded with a curse. We don't know her exact words,
but the man took just a few steps further on his journey before fall-
ing down, seemingly bewitched. His arms went limp, his speech fal-
tered, and his face drooped. (It is generally agreed in hindsight that
Law suffered a stroke). Alizon was convinced that her words had
directly resulted in the injury to John; she later confessed that her
curse had caused the injury and begged forgiveness.

This was the beginning of the Pendle witch trials and a complex
web of family feuds. Alizon Device confessed her guilt and also accused her grandmother, Elizabeth Southerns (known as Old Demdike) and members of another family, of witchcraft. She accused
Anne Whittle, known as Old Chattox, of murdering men by witchcraft, including Alizon's own father. In turn Anne Whittle accused
her own daughter Anne Redferne of making clay figures which she
used to practice witchcraft.

So, Alizon and Demdike were arrested along with Chattox and
Anne Redferne. Both Demdike and Chattox were in their eighties at

this time, with failing sight. They both admitted to selling their souls to the devil. With three admittances of guilt, all four women – Elizabeth Southerns, Alizon Device, Anne Whittle and Anne Redferne, were taken to Lancaster Castle and held in the dungeon to await an official trial at the next assizes, Elizabeth Southerns did not survive the cold, damp cells and died awaiting her trial.

In her 'confession', Elizabeth Southerns told of an experience she had twenty years previously. As she was coming home from begging, she passed a stone pit in the Pendle Forest, she encountered a spirit in the shape of a boy. He told her that if she would give him her soul, she should have anything she desired, including skills in magic. He gave his name as Tibb and became her spirit familiar and would reappear several times, often years apart, during Elizabeth's life, in various forms, including that of a brown dog, hare and black cat.

But this was not the end of the story. In April 1612 on Good Friday, Elizabeth Device gathered a meeting at Malkin Tower.* A meeting (or a coven of witches depending on who's telling the story) which would see more souls arrested and executed for the crime of witchcraft. Malkin Tower was the home to Demdike, her daughter Elizabeth Device and her children, Alizon, James and Jennet. The gathering that was held at Malkin Tower was *allegedly* to plan the destruction of Lancaster Castle and murder of the gaoler with witchcraft, in an attempt to free the incarcerated women. Word of this infamous meeting spread and shortly after, many of those who attended were accused of crimes of witchcraft and sent to join the others in Lancaster Castle. This included the remainder of Demdike's family, all apart from the nine-year-old Jennet, as well as others from nearby towns and villages.

The trials took place from 18-19 August 1612. The accused were denied witnesses to plead their innocence, and on 20 August 1612

---

* Mentions of Malkin Tower suggest it was within the Forest of Pendle and by Pendle Hill, within the ancient Forest of Bowland. But it has long since been reclaimed by the land, and probably the decay was assisted by locals still fearful of the place.

ten were hanged on Gallows Hill in Lancaster, including Elizabeth Device (who was accused by Jennet, her daughter, who would be the only surviving member of the Device family) and her children James and Alizon Device; Anne Whittle, and Anne Redferne. The others that would hang that day were Jane Bulcocke and her son John Bulcocke, Alice Nutter, Katherine Hewytte and Isabell Robey.

Fear of the covens of Pendle would endure for centuries to come – and the true sad history of the witch hunts that were fuelled by squabbles, fear and superstition turned, in time, into enduring folklore. Various regional protective rituals emerged as a result, in order to guard oneself from the witches that were rumoured to still roam Lancashire. The stories told that great gatherings of witches assembled on Halloween in the Forest of Pendle and the infamous Malkin Tower where the Devices had lived (the actual gathering many were arrested for took place on Good Friday, but clearly Halloween makes for a better superstition). It was said that one must carry a lighted candle about the hills between eleven and twelve o'clock on Halloween night, without it being extinguished in order to be safe from witchcraft during the coming year (witches would, of course, employ their utmost efforts to snuff the light). This was called "lating the witches".

HUNTING FROM THE WITCHES HORSEBLOCK ON HALLOWEEN

I found this story in Strange Pages from Family Papers *by TF Thiseldown-Dyer (1895). It is a fascinating mix of history, (with mention of the magic of the Pendle witches, though Mother Helston was not one of the accused), folklore and social commentary (what a woman may be pushed to do – become a wild deer – to avoid an unwanted marriage).*

It was said that Lady Sybil of Yorkshire was of unrivalled beauty and wealth. Scarcely a day passed without some fresh admirer seeking her hand. But she was in possession of high intelligence and her own interests, and far preferred to be free to walk the countryside she loved so much, and further her studies of nature. She was particularly fond of visiting the Eagle's Crag – also nicknamed the "Witches' Horseblock," to admire the surrounding views. And she had ambitions beyond her love of nature: she longed for supernatural powers and to take part in the nightly revelries of the famous Lancashire witches. So, as one does, she sold her soul to the devil and became mistress of the county, the Queen of the Lancashire witches, with skills to transform at will into a white doe.

Now, Lord William had long been a suitor for the hand of Lady Sybil and couldn't quite believe his proposals had been continually rejected. So, while Lady Sybil sought power and magic, he also consulted a Lancashire witch, Mother Helston, who promised him success on the ensuing All Hallows' Eve (clearly, she had little loyalty to Lady Sybil).

In the dusk of All Hallows' Eve, Lady Sybil was enjoying the countryside excursion in her doe form. Following the witch's directions, Lord William went out hunting, with his dogs and the hound familiar of Mother Helston, and they captured the white doe. The apprehended doe became Lady Sybil once more, her powers of witchcraft were lost, and she and Lord William were wed. But removed from her diabolical practices, Lady Sybil's health rapidly declined, her desires lost, and she died. Her grave was dug at Eagle's Crag. And it is here each year on the eve of All Hallows, the milk-white doe and the witch hound meet, and once more she must run for her freedom.

DANCING IN DARK FORESTS: WITCH TRIALS IN GERMANY

It was in Germany that more people were executed for witchcraft than anywhere else in the world. Friedrich Spee, a German opponent of the witch hunts,* called Germany "the mother" of many witches. The regions that suffered the most trials and executions were the territories governed by Catholics such as Bamberg, Würzburg, Mainz and Cologne. In each of these small territories several hundred (some estimate over a thousand) women, men and children were brutally tortured and executed, usually by being burned at the stake.

In German witch trials, as with many in Europe, alleged witches were sometimes accused of transforming into animals, such as cats or wolves, in order to carry out malevolent acts. Accused witches who were knowledgeable about herbal remedies and potions, often had this twisted against them, to suggest the use of herbs and plants for malevolent purposes, blamed for causing storms, lightning and other natural disasters through their supposed magical abilities. And perhaps most famously for the witches of Germany, they were accused of attending nocturnal gatherings known as witches' sabbaths, where they were believed to engage in rituals, dances and other activities associated with witchcraft and the Devil, in places such as the dark realms of the dark forests and the high mountains of the Brocken…

The stories of German witches intertwine history, folklore and fairy tales. The Black Forest in southwest Germany is renowned for its dense conifer trees, which contribute to its reputation as a dark and mysterious place often associated with fairy tales. This forest served as both the inspiration and setting for many of the fairy tales of the Brothers Grimm. The Harz Forest, located in northern Germany, also boasts a rich fairy tale heritage. It is believed that "Snow White

---

* In 1631, amongst the worst tortures and killings of the European witch-hunts, Friedrich Spee, a Jesuit priest, published a book called *Cautio Criminalis* speaking out against the trials as a cause of thousands of innocent people meeting horrific deaths.

and the Seven Dwarfs" drew inspiration from the Harz Mountains and the miners who worked there. The highest peak in the Harz region is the Brocken, which was considered a site of witchcraft and witches' gatherings, particularly during the May celebrations known as Hexennacht or Witches' Night. And a plateau within the mountain range is called the "Hexentanzplatz" or "the Witches' Dance Floor." In German folklore witches from all across Germany were said to fly to the Harz forest and the Brocken mountain on this night (named by Christians as Walpurgisnacht, in honour of St. Walpurga). Once there, the specific activities of the witches include: meeting with demons, celebrating and performing rituals on mountaintops, or dancing away the spirits of cold weather, snow and darkness to welcome the arrival of the Goddess of Spring.

The Harz region does have a pagan history. Sites of Old Saxon worship and pagan celebrations have been found during archaeological excavations, revealing altars used for animal sacrifices on the mountain tops, confirming at least some elements of truth behind the folklore. In present times, Hexennacht/Walpurgisnacht celebrations continue, as people gather to light bonfires, engage in songs and dances, and partake in festivities derived from pagan origins. And importantly, modern witches can now dance without the fear of persecution.

WITCH PYRES:
TORSÅKER WITCH TRIALS OF SWEDEN

On a wooded mountainside on the edges of Torsåker, Sweden stands a large stone memorialising the witch hunts that happened there, known as the Bålberget Memorial. The mountain is known as Bålberget (Pyre Mountain) or Häxberget (Witch Mountain). Though every witch trial and every accusation was a horror, some are just so catastrophic they stand out as symbol of how horrific the trials really were – in England the Pendle witches and the practices of the

Witchfinder General are two such examples. In Sweden a contender may well be the Torsåker witch trials. During 1674-5 in Torsåker parish, the largest witch trials in Swedish history occurred. In a single day 71 people were beheaded and then their bodies burned in the mountain borderlands between several parishes. Chaplain Laurentius Hornæus was extreme in his work of investigating witchcraft in his parish: 65 of his 71 victims were women (the remaining 6 were men and boys). This amounted to 20% of all women in the region. Three hundred years later, in 1975, the memorial stone was erected at the execution site. The inscription on the stone reads, "In 1675 witches' pyres burnt here. Women died; men judged. The faith of the times affects the man."

Often witch accusations spring up in times of hardship, and Sweden, especially in winter, was a harsh and cold place, harvests could fail and villagers grew hungry. So any neighbours who seemed to have better luck in harvest or milk yields, for example, could evoke jealousy and rumours – they may be accused as using demonic assistance. Some of the residents of Torsåker were Finnish, and something they did, that was different to the Swedish farmers, was growing crops within the forests around Torsåker. They burnt trees and grew crops in the ashes – which made for a rich growing medium and good harvests but earned them the title "the forest Finnish people". The Finnish were already 'other' and rumours rose of demonic help – and many of the people accused had connections to the Finnish settlers in Sweden.

But that wasn't the only reason women were accused. As was true throughout Europe, certain types of women were more likely to be considered suspect: those who might bless cattle for richer yields, who held healing knowledge, but also those considered stubborn, proud, or talked back to men. Like one accused witch known as "Finn Margareta from Fors," who clearly had a fighting spirit. Described as a "sorceress" who was "old as the hills",[13] when she was accused in court as being seen heading to Blakulla (a meadow of Swedish folklore where the devil held his wild parties) she ran at her accusers, and tried not only to beat them with her walking sticks but took out a knife she had been hiding and bit the hands of the peasants who tried to restrain her – as you can imagine, this didn't help her case, but I can't say I blame her!

So, this is all bad enough, but if you can believe, it gets worse. Because the witch trials in Torsåker largely relied on children as witnesses. In fact, many witnesses of the Swedish witch trials were children, as one of the main accusations of the 'witches' in Sweden was that they abducted children as part of their revelries with the devil, taking them to the Sabbath at Blakulla.

Like Jennet Device's pivotal role in the Pendle trials, children were the star witnesses as they retold tales of how they were abducted by witches, often children of accused witches themselves, the children would have grown up with tales of witch's abductions. But to get a "suitable" story, Chaplain Laurentius Hornæus had several methods to get children to give the testimony he wanted. Young boys were employed to point out those who had a 'witch's mark' and were paid for every identified 'witch'. Hornæus also threatened and tortured children to make them confess to being abducted by accused witches. His methods included plunging them into freezing lake water and for the smallest children, aged just four or five, putting them into ovens and threatening to light them; foreboding to them the flames of hell (there's a hell of an echo of "Hansel and Gretel" there – but it's no witch putting the kids in the oven, and it's well over a hundred years before the Grimms would put that tale into writing in the 1800s. You have to wonder if stories of putting children in ovens passed in whispers from such events). This man of the church, was guilty of the very things, and worse, that he was accusing the 'witches' of. Yet because he was male, and of the Church, he considered his actions just and virtuous.*

Few records of these trials remain, but in a small justice, the hor-

---

* When these rural trials were more closely examined by larger city courts, and these interrogation techniques were called into question, the disdain for the brutality was part of bringing the witch trials in Sweden to an end.

rors Hornæus committed were fully revealed by his grandson, Jons Hornæus, who recorded eyewitness and trial notes, published in 1771.[14] His work was called *Sannfärdig Berättelse (A Truthful Story)* and included the first-hand account of his grandmother, Britta. "I remember some of these witnesses, who by these methods were in lack of health for the rest of their lives". Jons adds that those children were still, decades afterwards, afraid to go near the house where his grandfather lived.

Something we see again and again is 'witch hunters' acting in ways far more horrifying and cruel that the accused witches ever were alleged to have done. And yet still, people use and think of the word witch as being the figure to be feared.

Unorthodox Religious Practice

Accusations of witchcraft could arise merely from someone being seen walking into forests, gathering herbs, or making charms from wood – leading to their arrest and trial as a witch. In 1644 Margaret Reid of Lanark, Scotland was accused of working with fairies and demons, practising folk healing, midwifery and unorthodox religious practice. "She did some compasses around babies spoke 'secret words', withershins with candles around the childbirth bed. Used a green hesp[†] at childbed ceremonies. Passed sick child three times round an oak tree."[15]

The carrying of rowan twigs, especially those tied with red thread (though a very common folk charm) could also be added to evidence that someone was a witch. In Scotland in 1618, Margaret Barclay was brought to trial for witchcraft in Scotland, strangled and burnt at the stake. One piece of evidence against her being that she carried a rowan twig tied with coloured thread in her pocket.

Two accused witches were tried in Scotland, sixty years apart, both accused of "Folk Healing" and "Unorthodox religious practice" us-

† Yarn.

ing rowan. In the trial of Issobell Watsonne in 1590, she was accused of and confessed to, healing a man using rowan wood (she claimed to have used a rowan and a piece of a dead person's finger for the cure). In the trial of Elizabeth Maxwell in 1650, she confessed that she passed a rowan over her own head to cure a sickness. (And also, though not related to rowan, a man became ill after he allegedly witnessed Elizabeth riding a cat!)[16]

TREE TALES: ROWAN (SORBUS AUCUPARIA)

Rowan is known in folk practice for its protective qualities against witches and fairies. Also commonly called Mountain Ash or quickbeam, throughout Europe, rowan's folk names include: witchwood, witches' tree, lady of the mountain, quicken tree, whispering tree, wildwood and its old Celtic name – *fid na ndruad* – means wizard's tree. In Scotland, the breeze rushing through the feathery leaves meant rowan earned the folk name "whispering tree" and it was considered a holder of secrets. It was often referred to as the Traveller's Tree because it was believed to prevent travellers from losing their way. Walking sticks made of rowan wood were considered to protect the wanderer from harm and in English folklore ships masts of rowan were highly regarded as they made a ship safe from spells.

Small crosses made from rowan twigs, each tied with a red ribbon (the colour red was, and still is, popular for protection against magic), were once widespread in the British Isles and worn by people and hung above doors at Easter or on May Day. Rowan boughs were laid across lintels, doorways and in stables for good fortune and protection from spells and witchcraft. Dried rowan berries can be threaded together to make protective charms, bracelets and necklaces (the red berries made the rowan berry a popular choice, though elderberries were used similarly).

MODERN WITCHES OF THE WILDWOOD

In Pendle, Torsåker and the dark German Forests, women and men were rounded up from poor, rural and isolated locations and tried for witchcraft. But what of those who *choose* to live in the forest... and actually identify as witches? By the mid twentieth century this was something people had more freedom to do, but they were still perhaps viewed a little suspiciously for doing so...

Simona Kossak

Ecologist and activist Simona Kossak (1943-2007), very much chose her wild home and loved a simple life close to nature. Some called her a witch as a result, but she was free to make such choices in the modern era. She spent more than thirty years living in a wooden hut in the ancient wildwood of Białowieża Forest.

> *"The little hut hidden in the little clearing all covered with snow, an abandoned house that no one had lived in for two years. In the middle room, there were no floors; it was generally in ruins. And I looked at this house, all silvered by the moon as it was, romantic, and I said, 'it's finished, it's here or nowhere else!'"*

Anna Kamińska, *Simona: The Story of Simona Kossak's Extraordinary Life* (2015)

She did her best to save the lynxes and wolves of Białowieża, re-moving any metal jawed traps she found in the forest.[17] But she went far further than most ecologists: Simona brought the wild into her home. A huge wild boar called Żabka lived in the hut with her. She raised deer and moose there, and sheltered rats, storks, foxes, lynx...any creatures that were in need or came by the hut were cared for, all whilst she fought for the protection of Europe's oldest forest.

Simona dedicated her life to the study and conservation of nature, seeing value in protecting biodiversity, and the preservation of natural habitats and ecosystems. She saw humanity as an integral part of nature rather than separate from it. Like the mythical figures we have met, she was, in her own way, a guardian and advocate for the forest and its inhabitants. Her wisdom and approach to conservation could well be seen as a contemporary manifestation of the wisdom attributed to forest-dwelling folk (and witches).

There is an iconic photograph of Simona with her "terrorist crow" companion, Korasek, that reminds me of another twentieth century woman who lived in the wildwood and openly claimed the title witch.

Sybil Leek

Sybil Leek (1917-1982) once described herself in an interview as "just an ordinary witch from the New Forest in England". Sybil was an astrologer and occult author who was known for her public persona as a modern-day witch and openly discussed her practices. She was an advocate of nature-based spirituality and living in harmony with the Earth and its cycles. Sybil's bird was a jackdaw – Mr. Hotfoot Jackson. There are excellent photos of Sybil with her bird familiar in the New Forest, with arms wide to spread her black cape behind her and Mr Hotfoot Jackson atop her head!

Sybil certainly saw her bird as a familiar – in various interviews and writings, she has mentioned her fondness for crows and ravens and how they played a significant role in her spiritual practices. She believed they served as messengers and guides between the physical and spiritual realms. For witches and practitioners of nature-based spirituality, crows and ravens have long been regarded as symbols of magic and intuition.

Sybil Leek was born from wild places, as she tells us in *Diary of a Witch* (1968). She clearly thinks fondly of this place, and in turn sees connections with her magical and wild nature with where she was born: *"in the classic place for witches, at a crossroads where three rivers also meet, a wild, desolate, witch-ridden part of Staffordshire.*

Three counties also meet there at the base of the Pennine Range... it is a tough, wild part of the country, with the blue-grey mountains dominating the landscape, where acres of heather make a purple carpet, where fairy rings are found." Like the mythical witch, Leek's beliefs and practices were rooted in a reverence for nature and the land, viewing it as a source of spiritual guidance and power, aligning her with the archetype of the Wise Woman living in the woods (or, as was actually the case, in a very charming village within an ancient forest).

Both Simona Kossak and Sybil Leek demonstrate their own connections to nature and a sense of stewardship toward the environment by their chosen way of life. And both may be seen as contemporary versions of the Wild Woman or "witch of the woods." Both exceptional women found inspiration, guidance and spiritual significance in their relationship with the natural world. Once you start looking, there is a wealth of stories of women and wise souls living in wild and wonderful ways.

Unofficial and Unconventional

The accused witches we speak of when we look at historical witch trials were often women who lived on the fringes of society – some were unofficial healers and herbalists, or those with knowledge of folk traditions – but that description could cover almost all women, and many men of the time! Almost all would have had at least some knowledge of herbs and a handful of family folk traditions like charms. And the pantries and kitchens of medieval and early modern houses were, along with food, stocked with tinctures and medicines, brewed using homegrown alchemy. But if these skills were combined with other variables – a low social position, isolated homestead, gender bias, a bad reputation, or having a particularly intolerant or fearful local clergyman – well, then you really could be in trouble. This is where any work of folk magic or superstition may well be named 'witchcraft', which suggests malefic intent.

This is also how it was possible that within the same thirty year period Nicholas Culpeper in his *Complete Herbal* (1653), advised curing "any scurf" using "the water that is found in the hollow places of decaying Beeches" and Hannah Woolley in 1675[18] – advised to "anoint your Visage well and often with hare's blood" to remove freckles, and to treat ear pain "put the wood of green Ash in the fire, and save the liquor that cometh out at the end". Trees (and hare's blood) are openly used in these household books, yet neither were considered particularly occult. But when others used trees in healing, they are accused as folk healers and therefore witch – in 1644 Margaret Reid was accused of practicing folk healing and taking a sick child three times round an oak tree. And in a trial of 1650, Elizabeth Maxwell was compelled to confess that she passed a rowan over her own head to cure a sickness.[19] (The fate of both these poor women is unknown.) It's hard to see the difference sometimes in accusation versus regular household practises, because there wasn't any, beyond the social standing, reputation, and often sex, of the practitioner.

Many of the women rounded up for trials lived in rural areas surrounded by wildwoods and natural landscapes, because that's where the peasants and poorer people were – away from the safety of towns. This isolation made them vulnerable to accusations and suspicion, these accused witches weren't necessarily living closer to nature by choice (though one hopes at least a few had such freedom – like Simona and Sybil choosing their beloved forest homes), using herbs and plants and trees was part of survival in this rural life.

I think it's fair to say that strong-willed and unconventional women are scrutinised more harshly than their male counterparts, simply for surviving (and hopefully thriving). For centuries media and literature have portrayed them as eccentric, unorthodox or even problematic due to their challenging of societal expectations. They may face more complex and gender-biased perceptions for what are considered 'unconventional choices'. This is something we will explore in the next section, as we turn our attention to the emergence of the Wild Woman archetype in contemporary culture.

6

WOMEN WHO RUN
WITH THE WOLVES

"Who knows where a woman begins and ends? Listen... I have roots; I have roots deeper than this island. Deeper than the sea, older than the raising of the lands...no one knows, no one can say what I am, what a woman is, a woman of power, a woman's power, deeper than the roots of trees, deeper than the roots of islands, older than the Making, older than the moon."

Ursula K. Le Guin, *Tehanu* (1990)

Perhaps every magical wildwood figure represents something within us that we can't quite put into words. So, we create stories and mythical beings and place them in the woods to help us find our way. From Eve to witches, jezebels to feminists, and every single woman who just doesn't 'know her place' or act in a way society considers ladylike, we love to tell stories that split good from bad.

"Wild uncontrollable nature was associated with the female. The images of both nature and woman were two-sided. The virgin nymph offered peace and serenity, the earth mother nurture and fertility, but nature also brought plagues, famines, and tempests. Similarly, woman was both virgin and witch: the Renaissance courtly lover placed her on a pedestal; the inquisitor burned her at the stake. The witch, symbol of the violence of nature, raised storms, caused illness, destroyed crops, obstructed generation, and killed infants. Disorderly woman, like chaotic nature, needed to be controlled."

Carolyn Merchant, *The Death of Nature: women, ecology and the scientific revolution* (1990)

The idea of witch emerged as a kind of counterpart to feminine ideals of the 'good', 'obedient', 'god-fearing' wife, the hard-working, uncomplaining, gentle mother, carer and homemaker. By contrast, women who refuse these roles or those who try to control their own fates reveal the contrary, self-assertive character of shrews, scolds, fish-wives, and of course, witches. This is why the realm for the bad woman was the wilds, far from her domestic sphere.

PARADOXICAL NATURE

Where Christianity and Western philosophy like to split the world in to good and evil, black and white, pagan cultures and the worlds of folklore and fairytale tend to allow for more ambiguity. Powerful forces and creatures are acknowledged as having two sides.

Nature, Mother Earth, the original goddess of duality, is both a life giver and life taker. This is the paradox and perhaps where the magic lies: in the acceptance that the wildwood and the witch are both things at once. Neither good nor bad, safe nor dangerous, but both and neither, all at once, great mother and the great destroyer.

Power, especially in the hands of women is something many within patriarchy fear, because power in the hands of the persecuted may well mean retribution and reckoning to their oppressors. Which we may see in the archetype of the wild feminine and her fanged smile…

THE WILD WOMAN ARCHETYPE

"We are all filled with a longing for the wild. There are few culturally sanctioned antidotes for this yearning. We were taught to feel shame for such a desire. We grew our hair long and used it to hide our feelings. But the shadow of Wild Woman still lurks behind us during our days and in our nights. No matter where we are, the shadow that trots behind us is definitely four-footed."

Dr Clarissa Pinkola Estés, *Women Who Run with the Wolves: myths and stories of the wild woman archetype* (1989)

The Wild Woman archetype is an embodiment of wild nature by a female: untamed, uncontrolled and disobedient – a stark departure from the societal expectations imposed on women as good wives, gentle mothers and obedient daughters. When a woman embodies this archetype she defies the conventional norms and rules set by her culture or religious beliefs, opting to forge her own path, against the approved ways set by societal expectations. Such defiance could well lead to accusations of madness, being a wild woman, a witch or possessed by demons (that represent the embodiment of everything that is not aligned with the divine or godly spirits). Throughout history, this portrayal of wild women as sinister beings has been used to instil fear and maintain patriarchal dominance, aiming to suppress the innate power and independence that such women possess, because women cannot, somehow, be trusted with power and knowledge in the way men are.

WHAT IS AN ARCHETYPE?

An archetype is a universal, recurring symbol, character, theme, or pattern found in myths, stories and cultures throughout history. These figures represent fundamental human experiences, emotions and traits and may serve as widely recognised elements in storytelling and the collective human psyche. Archetypes often transcend cultural and temporal boundaries, making them relatable and meaningful for many. They can include characters like the hero, the villain or the wise old mentor, as well as symbols like the journey, the quest or the battle between good and evil. Archetypes provide a framework for understanding and interpreting the human experience in literature, art and cultural narratives. We might connect the Wild Woman archetype to others such as the Wise Mentor, the Shadow, the Shapeshifter, the Threshold Guardian, the Warrior, perhaps even the Trickster or the Scapegoat, and certainly the Witch.

The Wild Woman archetype represents the instinctual nature of women, often painted as monstrous. We have already seen some of the connection between the forest-dwelling women and the wild beasts, how they are perceived and what they represent: in classical mythology, think Medusa, the Harpies, and the Furies. In fairy tales, the old woman in the woods, the witch and the cackling hag. And in folklore, it's the wild women of the woods who lure travellers astray. These wild ones are all partial vignettes of what it is to be a woman. Qualities that seemingly transform them in the eyes of society from woman to monster include: hunger, anger, rage, yearning and ambition. Perhaps in a patriarchal world which has had such a limited understanding of the feminine, we have been unable to properly articulate the fullness of what it is to be both woman and wild, so we use the sense of the trees, the magic and beings of the ancient woods (real and created) to help us craft a language beyond just words, but gilded with sense, feeling, intuition and deep-rooted memories and skills, as well as stories of careering and chaotic women, to express and explore this potential.

"An Aspen grove lives for a thousand years, the tongues of the leaves shaking in the wind. No aspen tree is just a tree, each is also a limb rooted into a much larger body that is an entire forest breathing together.

They called the old women crones, hags, cunning women, and witches. Names to make a daughter think she should devote herself to becoming something, anything, other than what she is. Like the women I descend from, the ones called hysterics and manics, obsessives and depressives, I feel as if I have an aspen grove that stretches from my stomach to my throat. Sometimes I can hardly speak for trying to hush those leaves."

Kathryn Nuernberger, *The Witch of Eye* (2021)

In more recent times, the archetype of the Wild Woman has been embraced by those seeking to challenge societal constraints, viewing her as a symbol of empowerment, liberation, and a reclamation of unleashed femininity. The Wild Woman archetype continues to serve as a source of inspiration and a reminder of the strength that can come from breaking free from oppressive structures and embracing one's true, unapologetic self.

Perhaps all of us feel a certain connection with the wild, and that within us is a wild creature filled with power and knowing. Society would have us all in rigid, 'civilised' roles, but what if we tire of this structure? How might we break free from roles that may leave us feeling trapped?

"I am a fascinating creature. I move in no stultifying ruts. There's no real yoke of custom on my shoulders… My Mind goes in no grooves made by other minds. It lives like a witch in a forest, weaving its spells, revelling in smooth vivid adventure."

Mary MacLane, *I, Mary MacLane** (1901)

Stories and mysteries, but also memory and instinct, may feel more real in the dark of the forest, the shadows cast by the canopy creating corners of darkness, and things just out of sight and unexplainable. Trees tower around you, and sounds, the owl hoot and crows calling in the silence of the forest, become magnified.

"The witch lives between dark and daylight, the safely settled village and the wild unknown of the woods beyond. The backlash years of the early 21st century revealed to many women something we had always suspected: we had never belonged to that daylight world. We had tried; we had worked; we had been loyal to the rules and values of society as we knew it. But, no matter how far we thought we had come, or how often our mothers told us we

---

*   Mary MacLane, a Canadian-born writer, known as "The Wild Woman of Butte" not because she lived in wilds, but purely for her reputation: she was considered scandalous, uncontrollable and wild.

could do anything, we still lived within a system that used female bodies as grist to maintain male rule. In the story that patriarchy told about itself, we were always going to be the villains. And if that was the case, we might as well make some magic out of it.

...

If the village didn't want us, we might as well head out into the woods.

Sady Doyle, *Dead Blondes and Bad Mothers: Monstrosity, Patriarchy and the Fear of Female Power* (2019)

A WILD WOMAN AWAKENS

"I call her Wild Woman, for those very words, wild and woman... the fairy-tale knock at the door of the deep female psyche... using words that summon up the opening of a passageway. No matter by which culture a woman is influenced, she understands the words wild and woman, intuitively."

Dr Clarissa Pinkola Estés, *Women Who Run with the Wolves* (1989)

In *Women Who Run with the Wolves* Dr Clarissa Pinkola Estés presented a ground-breaking body of work introducing the concept of the Wild Woman archetype to the masses who may never have been to a psychoanalyst before. By delving into the depths of female psychology and mythology, unearthing the ancient, and sharing the primal wisdom inherent in the Wild Woman archetype – an image that stands side by side with the witch archetype – Dr Estés presented as worthy and admirable, a female figure that was powerful and unruly, strong and intuitive, often strange, difficult and 'other'. It is an archetype that decades later continues to hold immense significance and resonance for many, many women.

Dr Estés presents a compelling narrative that empowers women to reclaim their innate strength, intuition and creativity, encouraging them to embrace their authentic selves and break free from societal constraints. In today's world, many women hunger for a deeper connection with their true selves – no mean feat in a world that still has so many rules for how women should be. For those with a yearning to rediscover the wild aspects of their nature that have been suppressed or overshadowed by societal expectations, the fairy tale stories that Dr Estés shares are like medicine. The Wild Woman archetype can act as a symbol of liberation and empowerment, a catalyst for transformation, offering a refreshing perspective that celebrates (rather than seeking to suppress) the wild aspects of oneself, and encouraging us to embrace our complexity and uniqueness. Her book offers a map, you might say, back to the wild, helping women to navigate the challenges of modern life and find healing through reconnecting with their primal instincts and knowledge.

To say modern life lacks the recognition and celebration of women's natural strength, emotional complexity and intuition is an understatement. In a world that emphasises conformity and adhering to predefined roles, many women find themselves yearning for authenticity and liberation from the pressures to conform, and the wild woman archetype is a beacon of inspiration for contemporary women and others seeking to break free. Dr Estés' profound insights and storytelling sparked a transformative movement, empowering women to embrace and reclaim their place as wild, empowered beings because, *"Bone by bone, hair by hair, Wild Woman comes back. Through night dreams, through events half understood and half remembered, Wild Woman comes back. She comes back through story."* And to find these stories we must *"go out in the woods, go out. If you don't go out into the woods nothing will ever happen and your life will never begin."* [20]

WOLVES AND GODDESSES

The work of Dr Estés really opened the eyes of many (mine included) to the power of these stories of the Wild Woman, and her connection to the wolf. The wolf can be seen as a symbol of the "wild" or unconscious aspects of the psyche, and stories involving wolf-women may reflect the exploration of these inner realms.

Dr. Estés provides glimpses into the inspiration that the wolf goddess and legendary wolf women offered to storytellers and devotees. This illustrates the essence of myth and the powerful messages it carries. It invites us to reflect on the parts of ourselves mirrored in these tales and consider the aspirations they awaken within us, shaping our vision of who we want to be and the kind of world we wish to create.

Connecting female figures with wolves has a long history; we've already met some in Section 4 like Žvėrūna-Medeina and the huntresses Diana and Artemis as connected in some way to wolves, hunting hounds and wild creatures. You'll also find the wolf goddess and wolf-women stalk through stories in many other cultures, embodying the wonderful dichotomy that goddesses can encapsulate so well: the natural world is both fierce, brutal, independent and strong, and nurturing, wise and maternal like the 'wolf-mother'. We see this in the many fascinating myths that show the varied ways wolves and the feminine have been connected.

There are many stories that highlight the strength and independence of wolf goddesses, wolf women and wolf witches. These characters may challenge conventional gender roles and offer alternative models of power and agency, they might serve as guides through these transformative experiences. Their shapeshifting nature often represents the blurring of boundaries between human and animal, civilisation and nature, conveying themes of duality and the complexity of identity.

☾ Norse Goddess of Winter and giantess, Skadi. As goddess of winter, mountains and hunting, she is often depicted with a strong connection to wolves, symbolising her association with the wilderness and its fiercest elements. In the myths shared in *The Prose Edda* (1220), she married the sea god Njord. Njord's home was a bright, warm place on the beach. But Skadi could not bear to be parted from her own *Thrymheim* (Thunder-Home), which was in the highest, snowy mountain peaks, and rang with the sounds of howling of wolves, so, they agreed to split their time between the two realms in compromise.

☾ In Norse mythology, two great wolves – Skoll and Hati – spend their days pursuing the sun and the moon across the skies. Skoll chases the sun goddess, Sól, in her shining chariot across the sky and Hati chases the moon god, Mani, during the night – in a perpetual cycle of day and darkness. It is foretold, however, that the wolves will, one day finally catch their prey, plunging the world into darkness, marking the beginning of Ragnarok (a cataclysmic battle that ultimately leads to the rebirth of the world). The mother of these wolves is a giantess or witch who dwells in a wood called *Jarnvidr* (Iron Wood).

> *"A witch dwells to the east of Midgard, in the forest called Ironwood: in that wood dwell the troll-women, who are known as Ironwood-Women [járnviðjur]. The old witch bears many giants for sons, and all in the shape of wolves; and from this source are these wolves sprung.*

Snorri Sturluson, *Prose Edda* (1220)

☾ The Celtic goddess Morrigan, associated with war, fate and transformation, shares a connection to wolves through her shape-shifting abilities and her role as a portent of battle – she also takes the form of crow and cow. In some tales, she appears as a wolf to attack those who have wronged her, in others she appears on the battlefield in the form of a wolf, symbol of the death and carnage to come...

☾ The wolf is held in great reverence in Native American culture. In Native American folklore, the legend of the Wolf Woman is rich and varied across different tribes. In some versions, a woman becomes a wolf to protect or guide her people. The Wolf Woman may serve as a symbol of balance and harmony between the human and animal realms, reflecting the indigenous belief in the interconnectedness of all living beings. In others, the Wolf Woman is a kind and helpful spirit who helps lost travellers find their way home, bringing peace and healing to those sick or injured. Wolves can be seen as guiding spirits, teaching the people how to hunt, reflecting a mutual respect between humans and wolves.

Witch Wolves

The contrasting connections of women, witch wolves, and the woman as wolf are revealed in how folklore and legends can inform or fuel both empowerment and prejudice. The best stories may seek to encapsulate the duality of wolves, of women and of witches. Wolves are known for their strong bonds with their packs and their protective instincts, and in some myths, women who care for or transform into wolves may be seen as embodying these maternal qualities. But wolves are also fierce protectors; a dynamic that can be interpreted as a combination of both nurturing and ferociousness. Stories of women connected to wolves may symbolise the integration of these dual energies as creatures of the wild, but also a symbol of the irrepressible aspects of nature as well. Depicted in the wild and wolfish goddesses are embodiments of fierce feminine energy, mirroring this profound connection, showing women and wild folk as guardians of the untamed, the protectors of the wild places, and the keepers of the ancient wisdom.

In *The Book of Were-Wolves* by Sabine Baring-Gould (1865) we discover that:

"According to a Polish story, if a witch lays a girdle of human skin on the threshold of a house in which a marriage is being celebrated, the bride and bridegroom, and bridesmaids and groomsmen, should they step across it, are transformed into wolves. After three years, however, the witch will cover them with skins with the hair turned outward; immediately they will recover their natural form. On one occasion, a witch cast a skin of too scanty dimensions over the bridegroom, so that his tail was left uncovered: he resumed his human form, but retained his lupine caudal appendage".

The Real Witchwolves of Estonia

"The Woman as Wolf" is one of the most popular folk tales and legends of witches in Estonian folklore – but is also very much part of the real history of the country. As in other countries of Europe, church law and folk belief is intertwined, and it is possible to spot some narrative motifs that clearly derive more from folklore than the material world.

Witches have long been connected to animals – many countries have lore about witches having the ability to transform or bewitch animals (as well as keeping them as mischievous animal familiars). In England, witches were thought able to transform into witch-hares and foxes; in Estonia and Latvia, it was wolves and bears, being the native animals of that landscape.

Estonian witchcraft trials reflect the folk belief in, and fear of, *werewolves*. Between 1527 and 1725 in Estonia, eighteen women and thirteen men were accused of changing themselves into wolves using animal skins or enchanting and riding wolves and causing harm to others as werewolves or witchwolves. The accused often confessed to being given their "wolf skins" by a person or a demon. In 1636, a woman said she was led into the forest by an old woman and given berries and sweet roots to eat; she then hunted with the woman in the woods as wolves. One husband testified that his spouse had turned into a wolf, and her female friend had taken the shape of a bear. The accused never voluntarily claimed to have had any association with devilry, but through leading questions and torture, the authorities drew out confessions about werewolves into admissions also, of witchcraft, which resulted in convictions and executions of the claimed werewolves as witches. A stone memorial stands in the parish of Viru-Nigula in Estonia for Kongla Ann, who admitted, (after torture), that she could shapeshift into the form of a wolf and hid her wolf skin under a stone. She was killed as a witch in 1640.

WOLF MOTHERS AND WEREWOLVES

The following tales are drawn from the story of the Swedish "Vargamor" in Benjamin Thorpe's Northern Mythology. Vol 2 (1851).

Here, once more we see strong consequences when a man – Lasse – does not show suitable respect and humility to the forest and her trees. The wild woman – the Wolf Witch – in the forest oversees retribution, and ultimately, through the good deeds of the man's wife, enables forgiveness and closure. An understanding seems to pass between the two women, who are unnamed in this story; they are simply – the good wife and the wolf witch. And there is a sense of fairness perhaps: once Lasse has served his 'punishment' and the wolf witch has received kindness of hospitality, Lasse is returned to his wife and cottage.

In a cottage within a forest there dwelt a man named Lasse and his good wife. One day he went out in the forest to fell a tree, but he did not offer the proper prayers before felling the tree and a Wolf Witch – a Vargamor – appeared, and transformed him into a wolf as punishment. His wife mourned for him for years, not knowing what had happened to her dear husband.

One Christmas Eve there arrived a beggar woman, poor and ragged, at the cottage door. The good wife gave her a kind welcome and shared food and wine with her. As she left, the beggar woman said that the wife may well see her husband again, for he lived, but walked the forest as a wolf.

The wife did not know what to think of this, but continued her chores and went to her pantry to prepare the meat for Christmas Day. When she turned to leave, a wolf stood before her, with sorrowful and hungry eyes.

"If you were my husband, we would be feasting on this meat tomorrow," she said. And in an instant the wolf-skin fell off, and her husband stood before her.

In Sweden, folkloric old women who dwelt in the forest were credited with powers of sorcery, and control of wolves. Thorpe includes a footnote to explain this term 'Vargamor', a word drawn from Swedish meaning something akin to wolf-mother/ wolf-crone in translation.

"Old women dwelling in the forests, who not unfrequently give themselves out as sorceresses, have got the name of *Vargamor* (Wolf-crones), and are believed to have the wolves of the forest under their protection and control. The heathen sorcery of transforming a person to the likeness of a wolf, is still believed by many to be transmitted to some wicked individuals, even to our days. Fins, Lapps and Russians are held in particular aversion on this account; and when, during the last year of the war with Russia, Calmar was unusually overrun with wolves, it was generally said that the Russians had transformed the Swedish prisoners to wolves, and sent them home to infest the country."

POWER AND PREJUDICE

Across global mythologies, stories of wolf goddesses, wolf women and wolf witches have emerged as potent symbols of the feral and instinctual, linked with wildness, embodying qualities like independence and transformation between human and wolf forms. As protectors of the wild, they traverse ideas of power and reflect humanity's intricate relationship with the primal. Whether feared for their unpredictability or revered for their courage, these narratives offer insights into the human psyche, our connection to nature and the interplay between civilisation and the wild.

Linking women with wild animals like wolves, could be seen as part of societies' attempts to confine them to traditional roles, perpetuating the idea that efforts must be made to ensure women are domesticated, obedient and subservient. The fear of women's potential power, both supernatural and societal, led to the persecution and execution of numerous women during witch trials, and all manner of trials since time immemorial. The witch wolf archetype can portray women as threatening and abnormal, dangerous, unpredictable beings, ever teetering on the edges of patriarchal control and that somehow, without the control of men, women would start devouring babies and running wild. I can't help but think of one of the many ridiculous things said by a television evangelist in 1992 in opposition to a proposed Equal Rights Amendment in the US that called feminism *"a socialist, anti-family political movement that encourages women to leave their husbands, kill their children, practice witchcraft, destroy capitalism and become lesbians."*

Both woman and wolf have been misunderstood by a patriarchal culture that tried to tame and/or eliminate them; presented and perceived as undesirable, a threat. The connection between woman and wolf is a powerful one for those rediscovering their inner wildness. Wolves once prowled through the British Isles but were hunted to extinction on these lands. It's believed they disappeared sometime in the eighteenth century, following, as RewildingBritain.org.uk puts it, "centuries of persecution". The wild woman and witch can surely relate. And how utterly fascinating and heartening it is that both witch and wolf were persecuted but as the wolf is being re-introduced to continental Europe as part of rewilding efforts, the witch too is growing, as an evermore popular claimed title of empowerment.

I rarely meet a woman (or magically inclined soul), when I say I write about witches, whose eyes don't sparkle a little, with an understanding that passes between us that either one of us could and would have been under suspicion once, and have felt shades of what it is to be demonised as women, and those considered 'other'.

Fear seems to distort traditional gender roles into wild extremes – creating an idea that if women are not carefully controlled, they will somehow transform from birthing children to eating them, from homemaking to killing their husbands. And a woman/wife outside of the home must be up to no good and is probably a witch – because you'd never find a good wife foraging for herbs, getting muddy, placing offerings for trees, or taking off into wild revels!

Through the lens of fear and patriarchy, woman as a wild hunter is a trickster, a wolf; a creature that stands on the edgelands, who cannot be trusted in her savagery. What could a wild woman freed accomplish? Patriarchal society may well be too afraid to find out. But that wolf is scratching at the door. And I think she is hungry…

To Be a Wild Woman

The Wild Woman archetype may be seen in all who dare to venture into the wilds within and without. These women, these seekers of the unknown, show us that the essence of the wild woman is not one of recklessness but of a courageous spirit to uncover the hidden truths that may lay cloaked in the depths of the wilderness. The wild woman is one who seeks the path less travelled. She knows that nature can be a teacher, healer, feeder, as is alluded to in so many tales of connection between women and the natural world, a bond as old as time itself.

The Wild Woman or witch is one who has learned to come into right relationship with qualities that have been demonised in women: hunger, greed, anger, selfishness, pride…traits that we have seen predominating in the witches of fairy tale and folklore so far in this book. The good Christian woman does not show any sign of these, the Wise Woman does not let them control her, but harnesses the power of these emotions, knowing herself as a force of nature, neither good nor evil, but powerful.

To be a wild woman can be to find connection with the rhythms of nature, to draw strength from the whispering leaves and the howling winds, to understand that the unknown need not be feared but embraced, for it holds the secrets of transformation and renewal. The wild woman knows that within the depths of the wild, one can find not only solace but also a profound sense of self. Stories we find of explorers of the uncharted, keepers of the wilds, and embodiments of the wild woman archetype, may well inspire us to venture into our own unknown, to run with the wolves, dance with the moon, and find our truest selves in the embrace of the wild…our wild.

THE MODERN WILD WOMAN

"What is wild cannot be bought or sold, borrowed or copied. It is. Unmistakable, unforgettable, unshakable, elemental as earth and ice, water, fire and air, a quintessence, pure spirit… Don't waste your wildness: it is precious and necessary."

Jay Griffiths, *Wild: An Elemental Journey* (2008)

The witch and the wildwood are still very much with us in rich contemporary forms of characters and archetypes. If the thought that women desirous of escaping domestic life for more rural pursuits seems like a very modern fad, books like *Lolly Willowes* published in

1926 – almost a century ago – suggests its appeal has been around far longer than current trends (although we may well be seeing a resurgence). In the fictional tale of Lolly Willowes – Laura 'Lolly' breaks free from a controlling family to live in the countryside and become a witch. In the centuries before this book was published by Sylvia Townsend, witch trial confessions that featured a figure of a devil often involved the offering of money, food and festivities as an escape to impoverished women, and those who felt constrained or controlled in some way. Sylvia's character Lolly shows echoes of being an alewife, hedgewitch and herbalist, she reads of witches, brews beer, publishes a book of simples and hedgerow healing herbs and has a fondness for mugwort. She becomes a 'wild woman' which to her family, is a terrible thing. Lolly's decision to move to a remote village represents her desire to escape the constraints of urban civilisation, restrictive gender roles and expectations.

Many of us can relate to the yearning for a life that aligns with our true selves rather than conforming to societal expectations. The character of Lolly, like the many wild women before and since, seeks to 'break free' as Lolly says herself in the final pages of the book (to Satan, no less!):

"It's like this. When I think of witches, I seem to see all over England, all over Europe, women living and growing old, as common as blackberries, and as unregarded... what can there be but witchcraft? That strikes them real. Even if other people still find them quite safe and usual, and go on poking with them, they know in their hearts how dangerous, how incalculable, how extraordinary they are. Even if they never do anything with their witchcraft, they know it's there – ready!... And think, Satan, what a compliment you pay her, pursuing her soul, lying in wait for it... you say: 'I will give you the dangerous black night to stretch your wings in, and poisonous berries to feed on, and a nest made of bones and thorns, perched high up in danger where no one can climb to it.' That's why we become witches: to show our scorn of pretending life's a safe business, to satisfy our passion for adventure."

If what another author, Ray Bradbury says is true, that "a witch is born out of the true hungers of her time," then in *Lolly Willowes*, Townsend tells us more of the hunger of those who would be witches, women who long "to escape all that – to have a life of one's own, not an existence doled out to you by others". Lolly, like many women longs to run wild and claim her own title, and that title is witch.

Our inner wild woman or wild soul flourishes through connection – human, animal, plant, spirit. And the Wild Woman archetype is one that is closely related to that of the magic worker, the witch. She leads the way to a wilder and greener, more natural and magical spirituality. A nature-based religion may well return us to the origins of human spiritual vision, but it does not need organisations, buildings, hierarchies, or belief in a god. More and more of us choose not to label ourselves at all, or maybe we think of ourselves as spiritual but not religious. We need not believe in anything beyond the natural world, unless our own experience tells us otherwise. All we need is a receptiveness to the world around us in its myriad forms and an openness to the unexpected, the unexplained, and of course, the wild...

We are more aware than ever before of how socially constructed rules and expectations have diminished women and have seen where obedience has gotten us – harassed, ignored and belittled. Women have never been more ready to embody the anger and mythic monsters and become fearsome and voracious. The wild witches and harpies now begin to speak to us, their wrath entirely justified, and necessary.

The wild means something different to us all, the same goes for what it means to be a wild woman. If you are thinking that to be a wild woman you must live off-grid in a yurt, you don't (though many would be very happy with such a sanctuary). Wildness is a big and blurred idea, as is that of the wild woman. For some she is one who forages for her food in the woods, for others she is one who knows the names of the birds, or lets her lawn grow into wildflowers to feed the bees or loves to sit in the dark of her city flat so she can see the full moon shine in. Maybe she is the woman that laughs when she is told to be quiet, or ignores those who tell her to cut her hair short after the age of forty. We may have started this journey in the wildwood but we can bring the ideas of the wild back into to our homes, into our urban lives. If the idea of wildness and embracing it speaks to you, you are free to discover exactly what that means to you. Remember this is the realm of the unruly, the liminal and the magical. If you name your adventures wild, then that is what they are.

CLOSING

*"Write and tell stories about your adventures in the woods.
Humans have done it for as long as they have existed. We turn
the woods into words: trees into paper, paper into books."*

Lucy H. Pearce,
***Crow Moon: reclaiming the wisdom of the dark woods* (2024)**

How do I bring this book to a close? How can I gather up the wisdom from these many stories to bring us back home? Well, I go for a walk, I walk through the trees with the stories, the histories, the myths and the monsters, the trial notes, the women almost erased from history and many who were, and the scant words that remain. I find a bluebell wood, a favourite in spring, and because it's drizzling and there is a Coronation on the telly, there is not a soul around. The woodland floor bubbles with a froth of blue, thousands upon thousands of bluebells simmer over grass and under rhododendrons and maples in glorious pinks and corals, and amongst the fairy bells and the witch hazels – I walk and I think…

Does the witch in the wildwood exist? Is she 'real'? Who is she to us now?

Like any good story, when asked if it is true, one may answer, "both: yes and no". The wildwood witch both does exist…and does not… She is fictional *and* real. Wholly appropriate, you might say, for one who travels in such liminality and in-betweens.

Folk traditions handed down through generations from times when magic was part of daily life. But also, that some of the accused were people carrying on traditions of healing, herbalism, divination and spirituality from pre-Christian eras, communing with the spirit of the lands and ancestors, fairies, nature spirits and other remnants from a distant past – a past that would come to be seen as threatening to new world views. Anything could be, and often was, blamed on the Devil and his hand-maidens: witches. Many of the accused considered themselves Christian, but also believed in magic, and charms, perhaps offering up these skills to earn a little money – and were probably bewildered by suggestions that they were cavorting with demons. They, like everyone else, were simply trying to survive, all the harder in a past world often filled with famine and illness, and so hostile to women.

The wildwood and witch captivate us and permeate our myths with both delight and disquiet. The figure of the witch in the Western world was born from ancient myth, folklore and rural practices. The witch of the wood is a stereotype. She exists more in the realm of fairy tales and folklore…far more so than accused witches of history. But she continues to embody the unknown that we fear when we step into dark unknown places. She is a figure that still looms in story, as a warning, as a strand of memory. And her wildwood has played a role in lore through fairy tales and folklore. Though their role may have changed as civilisations have, still there is an enchantment that continues into the present day – as tales of dryads, demons and witches continue to inspire us.

Once the witch and getting lost in the dark woods were right up there with the common man's greatest fears. And many a fairy tale and folklore created witches and ghostly woodlands specifically to represent such fears.

Once upon a time… The witch was the baddie in many a story, the one to be avoided, the one to destroy. They were different, and for many folk tales, that was enough to be painted as evil. Sometimes I wonder if we, as a society, are the "baddies", the evil forces when it comes to terrible, selfish decision-making about how we treat the Earth. What we take from and demand from it, what we put into it, or even just apathy as we disconnect from its beauty and vital importance. Now, in the West, largely we no longer fear the witch. But we do still fear loss, hunger and lack, perhaps this is the point, to face fears that haunt us about our future: the future of our trees, land and of our planet. Now as never before we teeter on edges of drought, floods, wildfires, extremes of heat, potential of food shortages. We have a stark reminder that the planet owes us nothing and we have taken greedily for a long time…and haven't the fairy tales been telling us long enough, what happens to those who are greedy, selfish, ungrateful or cruel…?

Inspiring Change

Stories can be powerful tools for influencing and inspiring change – carrying cultural heritage and wisdom and passing down beliefs, values and traditions, preserving a sense of identity and community. Speaking to us of the past, while influencing the present and future. Stories set in the wildwood that evoke a strong connection to nature and the environment can serve as a reminder of the importance of preserving the natural world, promoting ecological awareness and creativity that can lead to innovative solutions to real-world problems and inspire artistic expression. Folk and fairy tales have long been allegories for social issues and injustices, they may inspire personal growth and encourage positive action. By tapping into the timeless power of storytelling, these tales can shape our beliefs, values and actions, making them valuable tools for positive change in society. Stories can act as guides. Laying down the stories of our own lives alongside mythical journeys, we may find new pathways, doors into wildness and freedom, portals to redemption, resurrection and renewal.

There is currently a resurgence of interest in the natural world and its many wonders for numerous reasons, not least a seeking of greater connection to the land by exploring its stories, deepening experience of a place, and to help us find joy, enchantment and gratitude in the free pleasures of woodland walks and forageable foods, when the cost of living continues to skyrocket. Some may also argue that we are at a pretty big turning point as connection, protection and respect for the earth and natural areas has never been more important – for all manner of reasons, including such fundamental issues to self and planet as wellbeing and climate crisis.

Today, the witch stands as a changemaker and wise one who is empowered, connected to the natural world and its processes. She reminds us all of different ways of being, seeing and knowing. The continued existence of witch myths acknowledge that science, technology, monotheism and capitalism do not hold all the answers: the witch and the wildwood fill a gap with something more, something else that we may find enchantment and inspiration in. And when we reawaken to the wild, perhaps we reawaken to ourselves: with the sun on our faces and placing our feet on the earth.

WILD ENTANGLEMENT

Perhaps to capture the magic of the wildwood is to look at all that can dwell between the trees, between dense roots and blue sky, seen through branches, between life cycles and timescales vastly different to our own human lives. To find space for the storytelling exploration of history, to retell stories of people and their struggles helps us explore our present and how we make sense of the past. Within the stories is space to reflect.

Writers, storytellers and fiction authors have all breathed new life into the creatures of the supernatural, unleashing them into the imaginations anew. Hollywood, too, has played its part in bringing werewolves, witches, fairies and gods to new life, awakening older mythic figures. These stories still give us much to think about and to think with: ways of asking and answering questions about what it means to be human. Images and characters that may inspire us – powerful women, unafraid of the dark, free to work their powers and skills. And in modern culture many of us have powers and freedoms to live how we wish and connect to others who feel the same. We can be inspired and find strength in connection and supporting others.

The journeys we have made through this book have asked us to meditate on living in this land as heirs to a past which still affects the ways in which our humanity is defined, experiencing love and desire, facing up to death and loss, interacting with the animals we live alongside, and acknowledging the elements of wild and primal that lurk within us. The many-faceted stories of the witch do well to encapsulate society's often troubled relationship with the natural world and the countryside (and our wilder selves) as places of ancient and wild power.

Maybe, just maybe, wonder is the key to this revival of the wild ways and seeing them in new light: wonder and enchantment with the trees and the wildwood, the respect that the witch demands. The natural world might be just the thing that can save us and reconnect those broken links. Few of us actively listen to the trees anymore, yet our connection with the wildwood remains, and some still celebrate a rich tradition that honours our connection with the seasons, the land and the community. Whatever our journey or path may be, stories such as these can remind us of what is possible, and what may come to pass – good and bad. In enchantment we may find new wealth in our lives, and in the world around us.

I say on the back cover of this book, "Surely, we can all bear a little more magic, and a little more wild in our days". I think the same can go for finding our roots and anchors in a place, wherever we might happen to live. Stories can be our anchors. For our local natural areas, we may feel we are rediscovering our roots or exploring our land with enchantment in nature and her stories. Whatever it is that remains, of the wildwood, of ancient lands, of witch history, we can find it in words. What remains is story.

REWILDING OUR STORIES

To rewild is to return a land to how it may once have been; rewilding is a process of restoration and protection of wilderness, recreating, as much as is possible, an area's natural, uncultivated state. But can we apply it to people and societies as well? The rewilding not only of place but also of people and of stories?

We live in a world of more: more cars, more roads, more houses, more people… It seems there is not so much room in there for more trees (although many people are making noble efforts), more plants, more deer, more wild. They seem to me to be mutually exclusive, which is a grim prospect indeed.

What can we do beyond rewilding the land we steward ourselves?

We can give voice to the wild; we can share stories and continue to be inspired and challenged by all the elements of the wildwood that the witch embodies (and vice versa); remembering that nature is all around us, we can connect to nature even if we are far from the wildwood, perhaps that is our doorway back to enchantment and seeing of magic.

Myths, fairy tales, folk tales, whatever we call them, are old and powerful, from those kindled around sacred fires through to those gathered and forged in ink. We are all storytellers. We were born to seek narrative. Our wild hunter-gatherer minds have always been shaped by our reading of cloud, deer-trod, paw print and branch tip, in them finding a pattern, a story, a warning. Narrative is what allowed us to survive the wilds and reminds us that fruit, grain and water are gifts. We need story; we need mythic wonder from which to forage inspiration, courage and hope. What if we lost all sense of wonder in that wild world? Perhaps we have cut out the voices of all wild things, lured by thinking we are alone and above as civilised humans. Perhaps we have lost the sense of stories and myths arising from the world and wood around us, its dancing leaves, its water flows, its season turn and its wren and robin songs? I think these stories nourish the corners of our hearts where wonder dwells, where the boundaries of the world are nothing but gossamer veils, and all things speak, feeding and rekindling our wild souls that hunger for wonder, that hunger for magic.

When we walk the ground, seeking stories, we may find our way like mist, curling around the sight and sounds of what we imagine or have seen before – the granite rock to the witch's face, the mighty oak to wild man, the mushroom ring to fairy dancehall. Stories and spirits decorate the land to try and explain it – the witches and wood nymphs, goddesses and goblins run alongside animal and artefact, history and healing. Folk tales are, perhaps, a spell of their own, shapeshifting, word-magic, antlered messengers from the wilds and ancient times. And maybe this is a winding, roundabout way of looking at things, unfurling inexplicably in the half-light by sharing stories of fairies, witches, would-be cannibal women, hauntings and transformation in forest and glade and grove. And of that strange and wonderful connection of woman, witch and wild. But what else can we do with what we have left but wander the wilds, retell the tales, rewild ourselves and regrow our sense of wonder?

Certain spiritual ideas may have faded from memory, ancient centres of wisdom crumbled, and the custodians of that wisdom scattered. In such times, folklore may help preserve knowledge. Endangered wisdom finds refuge in the symbolic folds of folk tales passed down through generations. Though we may, at times, only grasp the surface meanings of these stories, we preserve them by retelling them. Preserved for any who seek to delve and uncover more profound truths within worlds where animals speak, plants possess healing powers, and wise, wild women lurk in dark woods, ready to offer their guidance to those they deem worthy.

Here's the thing – the stories of the ghost that haunts a woodland, the tree that looks remarkably like a cackling witch and that may or may not have an accused one under its roots, or inspired writers to speak of Ents, elves and orcs – perhaps you think me over-romanticising to say their gnarled boughs tell their own stories, no less valuable than our own. As well as centuries of gathering their secret commonwealth of moss, insects, birds and beasts, they are truly irreplaceable. No matter how many new trees we plant, they will never have these same stories – with dear hope, they will gather their own, but unlikely will it be that a hare thought to be a witch once hid in its roots, even if it was only ever a rumour.

And what does the witch in the wildwood give us? She is an integral part of this spirit of place and enchantment of place. We have explored just a fraction of the magical resources of the woods. And how the witch often plays that same role in similarity or in pairing with the forest as a link to the supernatural, potential for disorder, and the ability to lead, mislead, inspire and educate travellers. Offering a liminal space helps the unknown and the *other* to emerge, an invitation to adventure and discovery. A place to play, to think, to breathe deep and a place that offers infinite story. The witch and the wild can be magical; they can also be a commonplace part of everyday life. Their stories have been woven together for so long they are inescapably intertwined – maybe the witch will always, among other things, represent the wild possibilities of life and life within the wild. I do hope so.

So, if you should ever feel lost, walk. Walk the lost lands where our ancestors walked: the shaded corners, the wildwoods and the winding forest paths. Walk to the whispers in the scattered sunlight, mottled branches and crumbling earth of the wild others in their many incarnations. Walk to meet with far older, far wilder wisdom. And listen. We can discover magical stories, both old and new, if we are prepared to hear. And perhaps we can do our own part to preserve or revive local stories for trees, meadows, little corners of green and the great wild spaces. We can rekindle our connection with nature and our own sense of the special and the sacred. The world will always be complicated and, therefore, magical.

Humans have always found webs of enchantment and stories hanging in the trees; the natural world always has been, and hopefully always will be, filled with magic. The many stories of the witch are just part of a library of wonders held within ancient wildwoods. So, it must surely be wise to tread softly and listen carefully in honour of all our ancient stories and the immeasurable magic that dwells within them.

GLOSSARY & TIMELINE

People and Ages of the British
Isles and Europe

The British Isles are a mix of Celtic, Anglo-Saxon, Roman, and Viking/Norse cultures. So, we have an amazing collection of monuments, artefacts, deities, stories and folklore from ancient Celtic, pagan, Christian, Norse, Roman, and Germanic beliefs (as well as our most recent native religion, Wicca).

In order to bring some of what I have said into context it seems important to include a very rough outline. So, using the Encyclopaedia Britannica as my touchstone, this is an outline of five main historical eras: Ancient History, Classical, Middle Ages, Early Modern, and Modern eras. (You will see these dates vary wildly from different sources and for different places.)

Ancient History The Stone Age began about 2.6 million years ago, and lasted until the Bronze Age began. Being such a long period, it's divided into three respective periods: the Palaeolithic, Mesolithic and the Neolithic. What we consider to be modern humans, Homo sapiens, appear in the Palaeolithic period.

2500 BCE The Bronze Age.

1000 BCE The Iron Age which lasts up to the Roman invasion of Britain.

43 CE to 410 CE Roman Britain. Followed by a short period of time where the Germanic tribes that we could collectively call the Anglo-Saxons begin to arrive in Britain.

500 to 1400/1500 CE The Middle Ages, also known as Medieval, and I have used them interchangeably throughout the book. (Viking invasions came and went in this era, the Anglo-Saxon era ended too. And this was also the beginning of many centuries of European witch hunts.)

1500-1837 The Early Modern Era. Tudor, Stuart and Georgian periods respectively, this period also includes the Age of Enlightenment and the rise of modern science, and saw the official end to the European witch hunts.

1837-1914 Victorian and Edwardian eras, times of massive industrialisation and urbanisation in England and the expansion of Empire.

Modern Era The 1900s and beyond.

PEOPLE

Celts and Gaels: Celt is a broad term applied to a group of Iron Age tribes spread across Europe and the British Isles from their homeland in south-central Europe from around 1200 BCE. It was the ancient Greeks who created the word Celt, using it to refer to anyone in Europe north of the Mediterranean. From the word *keltoi* (meaning barbarian).

There are a variety of languages/groups that live under the Celtic umbrella: including Gaelic (Irish and Scottish versions), Cornish, Welsh, Manx, Briton and Breton.

Scotland, Ireland, and the Isle of Man are allied as Gaelic, joined together by common Gaelic language and cultures, and natives may refer to themselves as Gaels. With invasions of the Romans and the Germanic tribes, Celts got pushed out to the edges of Britain, so now when we think of Celts, it's the native languages and culture in Ireland, Scotland, the Isle of Man, Wales, Cornwall and a little of northern France. Celtic tradition was primarily verbal, so there's little documentation of the culture, but artefacts, carvings and burial sites offer us clues.

Druids: Members of the learned class among the ancient Celts, often priests and teachers. The earliest known records of the Druids come from 300 BCE. Their name has various etymological connections to the oak tree, so translations usually come up as 'knower of the oak' or 'oak seer.'

Anglo-Saxon: The Anglo-Saxons were members of the Germanic peoples from areas we know today as Denmark, Netherlands and Northern Germany; people known as the Angles, the Saxons and the Jutes all came together to form the Anglo-Saxons. They settled in territories that are today part of England and Wales, from the end of Roman rule up to 1066. We would describe these tribes as mainly pagan and they followed a Germanic pantheon of gods similar to beliefs that ran through Scandinavia.

Pagan: The term *paganus* is a derivative of the Latin word *pagus*, meaning "rustic", so those fancy-pants city dwellers might refer to someone who lives in the countryside as paganus! The term pagan later became associated with someone who followed ancient, primal, pre-Christian religions – Pagan is essentially just a blanket term for people who lived in Europe before the arrival of Christianity. It was often used to refer to anyone who believed in a pantheon of gods rather than one God. Witchcraft and paganism are often linked together as many witchcraft practices draw from pagan practices and vice versa. "Heathen" originally referred to Germanic paganism: the Heathens were the pre-Christian Northern European peoples, including in Anglo-Saxon England, Scandinavia and Germany. People from Celtic roots may self-identify as pagan. Whereas those who follow more Germanic/Norse may refer to themselves as "heathen," which, like pagan, is connected to country-folk meaning "heath dweller."

Wicca: A religion native to England created around the 1940s and 50s. Followers of this religion call themselves witches. The word "wicca" is from Old English roots and meaning "to weave/bend" and was later used to refer to a witch or worker of magic. There are, however, like lots of religions, many splinter Wiccan groups all over the world: Gardnerian Wicca, Alexandrian Wicca, Dianic Wicca – with many conflicting and contrasting views.

Witches & Witchcraft: To work with magic is an ancient idea and practice, and around the Middle Ages the term *witch* and *witchcraft* were applied to the practice (not usually as a positive). It is a title some can more openly claim today if they wish. You may also come across witches that are so named for their following of the Wiccan religion, not all witches do. The practice of witchcraft is far older than Wicca, and Wiccan practices are often drawn from these older witchcraft and folk magic practices. Pagan and witch are not necessarily the same thing, although they overlap: and one can be both; and can, but may not necessarily include a complex mix of religions, old and new, that centre on deities of pre-Christian Europe.

BIBLIOGRAPHY

Wild Magic

Natural Magic – Doreen Valiente

Letting in the Wild Edges – Glennie Kindred

Walking with Trees – Glennie Kindred

Where the Forest Murmurs: Nature essays – Fiona Macleod (nom de plume of William Sharp.)

The Folk-lore of Plants – T. F. Thiselton-Dyer

Plant Lore, Legends, and Lyrics – Richard Folkard

Old English Herbals – Eleanour Sinclair Rohde (1922)

If Women Rose Rooted – Sharon Blackie

Somerset Folklore – Ruth L Tongue

Ancient Art and Ritual – Jane Ellen Harrison (1913)

The Mythic Forest, the Green Man and the Spirit of Nature – Gary Varner

Nature's Ways: lore, legend, fact and fiction – Ruth Binney

In our Nature: Stories of Wildness – compiled by Donna Seaman

Stories of the Land

Handbook of Folklore – Charlotte Sophia Burne

The Mabinogion – Lady Charlotte Guest

Discovering the Folklore of Plants – Margaret Baker

Folktales of Norway – Reidar Thorwalf Christiansen

Folktales of England – Katharine Mary Briggs and Ruth L Tongue

Tree Talk: memories, myths and timeless customs – Marie-France Boyer

The Green Man – companion and gazetteer. His origins, his history, his folklore, his meaning and where to find him – Ronald Millar

Gossip from the Forest: The Tangled Roots of Our Forests and Fairy Tales – Sara Maitland

Landscape & Memory – Simon Schama

The Forest and the EcoGothic: The Deep Dark Woods in the Popular Imagination – Elizabeth Parker

The Stories of the Trees – Mrs. S.L Dyson

Forests: The Shadow of Civilization – Robert Pogue Harrison

Wildwood: A Journey through Trees – Roger Deakin

The Wild Places – Robert Macfarlane

Whispers from the Woods: the lore & magic of trees – Sandra Kynes

To Speak for the Trees: My Life's Journey from Ancient Celtic Wisdom to a Healing Vision of the Forest – Diane Beresford-Kroeger

Folklore in Lowland Scotland – Evelyn Blantyre Simpson (1908)

The Land of the Green Man: a journey through the supernatural landscapes of the British Isles – Carolyne Larrington

Witchcraft and Magic in Europe: The Period of the Witch Trials – Bengt Ankarloo & Stuart Clark

Witchcraft and Magic in Europe: Ancient Greece and Rome – Valerie Flint et al.

The Fairy-Faith in Celtic Countries – Walter Evans Wentz

Religions of Rome: A Sourcebook – Mary Beard, John North, and Simon Price

Wild Woman & Witch

Diary of a Witch – Sybil Leek

Woman and Nature: the Roaring Inside Her – Susan Griffin

Braiding Sweetgrass: Indigenous Wisdom, Scientific Knowledge and the Teachings of Plants – Robin Wall Kimmerer

Writing Wild: Women Poets, Ramblers, and Mavericks Who Shape How We See the Natural World – Kathryn Aalto

The Death of Nature: women, ecology and the scientific revolution – Carolyn Merchant

Women on Nature: 100+ Voices on Place, Landscape & the Natural World – Katharine Norbury

A History of Magic and Witchcraft: Sabbats, Satan and Superstitions in the West – Frances Timbers

From the Beast to the Blonde – Marina Warner

Folk-lore and Folk-stories of Wales – Marie Trevelyan

Cunning Folk and Familiar Spirits: Shamanistic Visionary Traditions In Early Modern British Witchcraft and Magic – Emma Wilby

Riding the nightmare: Women & Witchcraft – Selma R Williams

Witchcraft in Europe, 400-1700: a documentary history
– Alan Charles Kors and Edward Peters

The Book of Were-Wolves – Sabine Baring-Gould

Fearless Wives and Frightened Shrews: the construction of the witch in early modern Germany – Sigrid Brauner

Witches, Witch-hunting, and Women – Silvia Frederici

A History of Magic, Witchcraft and the Occult – Suzannah Lipscomb

The Lancashire Witches: histories and stories – Robert Poole

Crow Moon: reclaiming the wisdom of the dark woods – Lucy H. Pearce

A Source Book of Scottish Witchcraft – Christina Larner

Pamphlets from the era of the witch trials

"The Wonderful Discoverie of the Witchcrafts of Margaret and Phillip Flower" (1618)

"A true and exact relation of the severall informations, Examinations, and Confessions of the late Witches, arraigned and executed in the County of Essex" (1645)

"A most wicked worke of a wretched Witch, (the like whereof none can record these manie yeeres in England.)" (1592)

"A true and iust recorde, of the information, examination and confession of all the witches, taken at S. Ofes in the countie of Essex" (1582)

"The Wonderfull Discoverie of Witches in the Countie of Lancaster"
– Thomas Potts (1613)

Essays & Articles

"Turning our Fairy Tales Feral Again" – Sylvia Lindsteadt

"The Contemporary Witch, the Historical Witch and the Witch Myth: The Witch, Subject of the Appropriation of Nature and Object of the Domination of Nature" – Silvia Bovenschen

"Reading Witches, Reading Women: Late Tudor and Early Stuart Texts"
– Jennifer A. McGowan

"Herodias the Wild Huntress in the Legend of the Middle Ages"
– Waldemar Kloss

"They Ride on the Backs of Certain Beasts:" The Night Rides, the Canon Episcopi, and Regino of Prüm's Historical Method" – Chris Halsted

"New Outlook for Zvėrūna-Medeina" – Vykintas Vaitkevičius

"Witches, Wives and Mothers: witchcraft persecution and women's confessions in seventeenth-century England"
– Louise Jackson, *Women's History Review,* 4:1, (1995)

Fairy Tales & Folklore

Jacob and Wilhelm Grimm: Household Tales – translated by Margaret Hunt (1884)

The Fairy Tales of the Brothers Grimm – translated by Mrs Edgar Lucas (1911)

A Book of Witches – Ruth Manning-Sanders

The Three Witch Maidens – Ruth Manning-Sanders

The Green Forest Fairy Book – Loretta Ellen Brady

The Old, Old Fairy Tales – Laura Valentine (1899)

The Other Side of the Sun: Fairy Stories – Evelyn Sharp (1900)

Top of-the-World Stories for Boys and Girls – Emilie Poulsson and Laura Poulsson (1916)

The Book of Nature Myths – Florence Holbrook

The Green Forest Fairy Book – Loretta Ellen Brady

The Forest in Folklore and Mythology – Alexander Porteous

Woodland Folk Tales of Britain and Ireland – Lisa Schneidau

Courting the Wild Twin – Martin Shaw

Folk Belief and Traditions of the Supernatural – Tommy Kuusela and Giuseppe Maiello

The Russian Story Book – Richard Wilson

Fairy Tales of the Slav Peasants and Herdsmen – Alexander Chodzko

Clan Traditions and Popular Tales of the Western Highlands and Islands – John Gregorson Campbell

The Land Beyond the Forest: Facts, Figures, and Fancies from Transylvania – Emily Gerard

The Wisdom of Fairy Tales – Rudolf Meyer
British Folk Customs – Christina Hole

Online Resources & Digital Archives

archive.org

britannica.com

witchesofscotland.com

Survey of Scottish Witchcraft Database – http://witches.shca.ed.ac.uk

treesforlife.org.uk

Folklore Archive of the Finnish Literature Society in Helsinki: www.finlit.fi

USC Digital Folklore Archives: folklore.usc.edu

The 'Gallica' Archives: gallica.bnf.fr

The Harvard digital collections: library.harvard.edu/digital-collections

The Beinecke rare book and manuscript library: beinecke.library.yale.edu

ENDNOTES

1   *The Spirit of Trees: science, symbiosis and inspiration*, Fred Hageneder (2000)

2   *Domestic Folk-lore* – T. F. Thiselton-Dyer (1881)

3   Woodland Trust + National Park figures, correct at time of publishing.

4   *Encyclopaedia of Giants and Humanoids in myth, legend and folklore*, Theresa Bane

5   *Dictionar De Mitologie Romana*, Ion Ghinoiu

6   *An Encyclopedia of Fairies Hobgoblins, Brownies, Bogies, And Other Supernatural Beings*, Katharine Mary Briggs

7   *An Encyclopedia of Fairies Hobgoblins, Brownies, Bogies, And Other Supernatural Beings*, Katharine Mary Briggs

8   A book created by English translator of texts, Lady Charlotte Guest. She published her translations of eleven medieval Welsh folk tales in seven volumes between 1838 and 1845. Many of the tales are much older in origin and drawn from texts such as *The White Book of Rhydderch* (1300-1325) and *The Red Book of Hergest* (1375-1425) and texts attributed to Taliesin, the Welsh bard.

9   As suggested by Welsh scholar John Rhys in 1886.

10   *New outlook for žvėrūna-medeina*, Vykintas Vaitkevičius, Lithuanian archaeologist.

11   If you want to read for yourself you'll find Mielikki mentioned in Runes (chapters) 14, 32, and 46 of The Kalevala which can be found online.

12   Found in Elizabeth Lynn Linton, *Witch Stories* (1861).

13   From the testimonies given in the District Court.

14   *Folklife* magazine article by Jennie Tiderman-Österberg and excerpts from *A Truthful Story* by Jons Hornæus from an excellent lecture by Maria Nordlund, archaeologist and researcher at the Västernorrlands museum, Sweden.

15   From trial records.

16   From the Survey of Scottish Witchcraft database, within which the fate of both women is unknown.

17   You can find many of these stories along with fabulous photos in the book *Simona: The Story of Simona Kossak's Extraordinary Life* by Anna Kamińska and online at culture.pl/en/article/the-extraordinary-life-of-simona-kossak

18   in *The Accomplish't lady's Delight in Preserving, Physick, beautifying, and cookery*

19   *A Source Book of Scottish Witchcraft*, Christina Larner (1977)

20   All from Dr Clarissa Pinkola Estés, *Women Who Run with the Wolves*

ABOUT THE AUTHOR

S arah Robinson is the best-selling author of *Yoga for Witches* (now available in French, Polish and Chinese), *Yin Magic*, *Kitchen Witch: Food, Folklore & Fairy Tale* which was featured in Cosmopolitan's top witch books and recipient of the Comfy Cosy Book Award 2022, and *Enchanted Journeys*.

Sarah is a yoga teacher and author based in Bath, UK. Her background is in science, she holds an MSc in Psychology and Neuroscience and has studied at Bath, Exeter and Harvard universities.

Website: sentiayoga.com
Instagram: @yogaforwitches

ABOUT WOMANCRAFT

Womancraft Publishing was founded on the revolutionary vision that women and words can change the world. We act as midwife to transformational women's words that have the power to challenge, inspire, heal and speak to the silenced aspects of ourselves, empowering our readers to actively co-create cultures that value and support the female and feminine. Our books have been #1 Amazon bestsellers in many categories, as well as Nautilus and Women's Spirituality Award winners.

As we find ourselves in a time where old stories, old answers and ways of being are losing their authority and relevance, we at Womancraft are actively looking for new ways forward. Our books ask important questions. We aim to share a diverse range of voices, of different ages, backgrounds, sexual orientations and neurotypes, seeking every greater diversity, whilst acknowledging our limitations as a small press.

At the heart of our Womancraft philosophy is fairness and integrity. Creatives and women have always been underpaid: not on our watch! We split royalties 50:50 with our authors. We offer support and mentoring throughout the publishing process as standard. We use almost exclusively female artists on our covers, and as well as paying fairly for these cover images, offer a royalty share and promote the artists both in the books and online. Whilst far from perfect, we are proud that in our small way, Womancraft is walking its talk, living the new paradigm in the crumbling heart of the old: through financially empowering creative people, through words that honour the Feminine, through healthy working practices, and through integrating business with our lives, and rooting our economic decisions in what supports and sustains our natural environment. We are learning and improving all the time. I hope that one day soon, what we do is seen as nothing remarkable, just the norm.

We work on a full circle model of giving and receiving: reaching backwards, supporting Treesisters' reforestation projects and the UNHCR girls' education fund, and forwards via Worldreader, providing e-books at no-cost to education projects for girls and women in developing countries. We donate many paperback copies to education projects and women's libraries around the world. We speak from our place within the circle of women, sharing our vision, and encouraging them to share it onwards, in ever-widening circles.

We are honoured that the Womancraft community is growing internationally year on year, seeding red tents, book groups, women's circles, ceremonies and classes into the fabric of our world. Join the revolution! Sign up to the mailing list at womancraftpublishing.com and find us on social media for exclusive offers:

(f) womancraftpublishing

(○) womancraft_publishing

**Signed copies of all titles available from
shop.womancraftpublishing.com**

ABOUT THE ARTIST

Olya Luki (real name Olga Lukina) is an illustrator and designer from Russia, living in the city of Krasnodar. She is engaged in creating illustrations based on Russian/Slavic folklore, history, depicting the diversity of her native culture and the riches of nature. She believes that we must not forget the culture of our ancestors and need to adopt the experience of older generations. Olya searched for a long time, more than five years, for her unique style in digital illustration, but now this allows her to stand out from the great variety of other artists. The artist is open to collaboration with people from different countries of the world, because she believes that even in the darkest times you can find bright people.

USE OF WOMANCRAFT WORK

Often women contact us asking if and how they may use our work. We love seeing our work out in the world. We love you sharing our words further. And we ask that you respect our hard work by acknowledging the source of the words.

We are delighted for short quotes from our books – up to 200 words – to be shared as memes or in your own articles or books, provided they are clearly accompanied by the author's name and the book's title.

We are also very happy for the materials in our books to be shared amongst women's communities: to be studied by book groups, discussed in classes, read from in ceremony, quoted on social media… with the following provisos:

☽ If content from the book is shared in written or spoken form, the book's author and title must be referenced clearly.

☽ The only person fully qualified to teach the material from any of our titles is the author of the book itself. There are no accredited teachers of this work. Please do not make claims of this sort.

☽ If you are creating a course devoted to the content of one of our books, its title and author must be clearly acknowledged on all promotional material (posters, websites, social media posts).

☽ The book's cover may be used in promotional materials or social media posts. The cover art is copyright of the artist and has been licensed exclusively for this book. Any element of the book's cover or font may not be used in branding your own marketing materials when teaching the content of the book, or content very similar to the original book.

☽ No more than two double page spreads, or four single pages of any book may be photocopied as teaching materials.

We are delighted to offer a 20% discount of over five copies going to one address. You can order these on our webshop, or email us at info@womancraftpublishing.com

Kitchen Witch: Food, Folklore & Fairytale

Sarah Robinson

Welcome to a place of great magic – the kitchen! Magic, superstition, cooking, and food rituals have been intertwined since the beginning of humankind. *Kitchen Witch: Food, Folklore & Fairy Tale* is an exploration of the history and culture of food, folklore and magic and those skilled in healing and nourishing – herbalists, wise women, cooks, cunning folk and the name many of them would come to bear: witch.

Kitchen Witch is an invitation to see the magic in every corner of your kitchen. With the Kitchen Witch as our guide, we'll explore food, nature, magic, and transformation. We'll discover what the name of Kitchen Witch could mean to us in modern interpretations of ancient practices. May this book of stories and ideas show that there's magic in the mundane, witchcraft within your walls and the Goddess really is in the details.

The Kitchen Witch Companion: Recipes, Rituals & Reflections

Lucy H. Pearce & Sarah Robinson

The Kitchen Witch returns in this beautifully illustrated companion book to Sarah Robinson's bestseller *Kitchen Witch: Food, Folklore & Fairy Tale*...

This is a book to be read curled up in a comfy chair, before being covered in earth as you gather in seasonal goodness and splattered with sauce as you cook! The first half of *The Kitchen Witch Companion* is a reflection on the fantasy and reality of making magic in the kitchen. The second half is a seasonal collection of recipes and crafts, foraging and ferments, spells and simmer pots, meditations and blessings to inspire you to create, celebrate and gather throughout the Wheel of the Year.

CROW MOON:
RECLAIMING THE WISDOM OF THE DARK WOODS

Lucy H. Pearce

Three-time Nautilus award-winning author Lucy H. Pearce's previous best-selling book *Burning Woman* was an initiation of fire, *She of the Sea* an initiation of water and *Crow Moon* is an initiation of earth and air, a way back to the heart of ourselves through wild revelation.

Strikingly illustrated by the author, with contributions from over thirty women – artists, healers, authors – midlife women who have also been called by the strange magic of crows at decisive moments in their lives.

WALKING WITH PERSEPHONE:
A JOURNEY OF MIDLIFE DESCENT AND RENEWAL

Molly Remer

Midlife can be a time of great change – inner and outer: a time of letting go of the old, burnout and disillusionment. But how do we journey through this? And what can we learn in the process? Molly Remer is our personal guide to the unraveling and reweaving required in midlife. She invites you to take a walk with the goddess Persephone, whose story of descent into the underworld has much to teach us.

Walking with Persephone is a story of devotion and renewal that weaves together personal experiences, insights, observations, and reflections with experiences in practical priestessing, family life, and explorations of the natural world. It advocates opening our eyes to the wonder around us, encouraging the reader to both look within themselves for truths about living, but also to the earth, the air, the sky, the animals, and plants.